52 REASONS
NOT TO VOTE FOR OBAMA

WRITTEN BY **ANTHONY HOLM** WITH A FOREWORD BY **HERMAN CAIN**

Velocity • MASCOT

New York

Requests for permission to make copies of any
part of the work should be submitted online
to info@mascotbooks.com or mailed to:

Velocity • Mascot
560 Herndon Parkway #120
Herndon, VA 20170.

ISBN-10: 1-62086-018-X
ISBN-13: 978-1-62086-018-2
Library of Congress Control Number: 2012934324
CPSIA Code: PRT0412B

Cover artwork by Danny Moore

Printed in the United States of America

www.mascotbooks.com
www.velocity-books.com

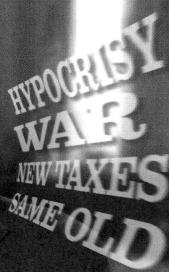

"This book is dedicated to Adam Goldston
from whom we can all learn what it means to
be courageous—presidents and paupers alike."

ACKNOWLEDGMENTS

Like most productions, this book would not be possible without the aid of so many others. Without their kindness and support, this book would not exist. My friends, family, fellow authors, publisher, and numerous others allowed this book to come to market. I am eternally grateful to all of you.

In particular I want to thank, the publishing teams at Velocity and Mascot Books; Herman Cain for his friendship; Alex Morris for his quips and insight; Carrie Simmons for her edits and aid; Andrew Barlow, a gifted wordsmith whose humility is a lesson for us all; Stephen Boane, whose curiosity and strong mind make him invaluable to any endeavor; and Peggy O'Shaughnessy, whose faith and love helped settle my mind allowing my voice to be heard.

Additionally, we all benefit from organizations such as PolitiFact, the Brookings Institution, the Heritage Foundation, and the mainstream media outlets whose information is publicly available online. These groups aid all of us in researching issues and bring new levels of transparency to government.

TABLE OF CONTENTS

FOREWORD

BY HERMAN CAIN

Anthony Holm is one of the most thoughtful and deliberative communicators, whose commitment to truth and liberty is unmatched. The book that follows is a reasoned analysis of Barack Obama's promises and pledges to voters juxtaposed with what our president actually did once elected.

Anthony and I, and millions of informed citizens, believe Barack Obama should not be reelected. There is an old adage that politicians will say anything to get elected, and *52 Reasons NOT to Vote for Obama* gives powerful examples of how Barack Obama did just that.

The smoke and mirrors of Obama's administration continues to provide false hope for the people of America. His policies desecrate the taxpayer and send much needed jobs overseas. His mandates encroach on the rights of every man, woman, and child and continue to burden federal and state budgets. All the while his endless spending provides no economic growth or job creation, sending our children and grandchildren into debt like no generation ever before.

We have had enough of his eloquent speeches, grand gestures, and small pandering programs that do nothing to solve our real problems; we must cut through the politically correct minutia and find solutions to the historic problems plaguing our country. It's the president's duty to honestly acknowledge our nation's problems and present credible solutions. The "solutions" I have seen thus far have only momentarily plugged the hole. The dam will burst, and the destruction will be devastating.

We must have a meaningful reduction in spending, throw out the tax code, and reduce the role of government in our lives.

It is time to seek a leader with the courage to say no and the audacity to make changes to a system in great need of renovation. The last three years have shown Mr. Obama is not this leader. He can no longer blame Congress or previous administrations for our current situation.

This book sheds light on the all-too-familiar, ugly side of politics and the truths that ultimately surface. Mr. Obama must be held accountable for his hypocrisies, deceptions, and failures.

America deserves more from our president, and more from all of our elected officials. We are a nation of the people, for the people; our current leaders seem to have forgotten those guiding words from our founding fathers. We must expose and remind them.

It is our duty to remind them that we are paying attention, we do understand, and we demand more. We have an obligation to those who fought to keep our nation free and endured pain and punishment to ensure our freedom and democracy.

It is more important now than ever before that citizens understand the magnitude of their choice in leaders. Let's not allow ignorance of the issues to be an excuse any longer. Stay informed, stay involved, stay inspired, and keep those around you educated. You must not just think of yourself but of the legacy you wish to leave your children and grandchildren, and of the world you want for them.

I admire Anthony's dedication to the truth and his passion for educating people on the facts. The future of our great nation resides in the hands of well-informed voters.

This book will help you to become that voter.

INTRODUCTION

"Politicians will say anything to get elected." "Politicians are all liars."

We hear these truisms more often each political season—so much so that they have transcended cynicism to become the standard expectation of all too many mainstream Americans.

But what does "say anything to get elected" mean? What does "they're all liars" signify? We all know that a candidate will occasionally say something he or she doesn't believe or change his or her position on an issue in order to help win an office. A candidate changing a position is not surprising; it's been going on since the country was founded.

Most presidents have at least one memorable example of when they changed positions or went back on their word in a way that merits the label "lie." President George H. W. Bush had his famous "Read My Lips: No New Taxes" moment, only to sign a bill into law raising new taxes. President Bill Clinton's famous example came when he said, "I did not have sexual relations with that woman."

So if presidents break their word once or twice, we're not surprised. We expect it. In most cases, we even forgive it. But how many times can a president reverse a clear position or break a stated promise before becoming something other than a standard politician?

When does "shifting positions" turn him into a hypocrite? When does "dissembling" make him a liar? Do we start mistrusting him deeply at five broken promises? Do we decide he's a hypocrite at ten? Is he an out-and-out liar at fifteen? What do we think of twenty-five lies? What do we think of fifty?

What follows is an unblinking look at fifty-two significant promises, pledges, and policy statements made by Barack Obama. Each begins with a quote that is presented *in context*, not in political "gotcha" fashion. And each stands in stark contrast with the actions and positions he has subsequently taken as president.

The difference between campaigning and governing will always cause shifts between what is promised and delivered. But how far can these disconnections go and still be tolerable? How much is too much? Where does the line finally get crossed from disturbingly normal to flatly fraudulent?

You'll have to decide for yourself whether fifty-two broken promises, reversals of policies, and clever misdirections make Obama a liar, a hypocrite, or simply another politician. Speaking for myself, these fifty-two examples become a parade of *52 Reasons NOT to Vote for Obama*.

GROWING ON TREES

MORE DEBT IN THE LAST TWO YEARS THAN IN THE PREVIOUS TWO HUNDRED

"...but actually I'm cutting more than I'm spending so it will be a net spending cut."

—Candidate Barack Obama

Candidate Obama took frequent shots at President Bush's role in our debt crisis when he was running against Democratic foe Hillary Clinton and Republican frontrunner John McCain. Obama attempted to portray himself as an improvement over Bush while implying that Clinton and McCain would bring more of the same deficit spending and increases in our national debt.

Candidate Obama claimed that his plan would produce a "net spending cut" on our national debt, which was just over $10 trillion when he took office.

Voters who were sick of profligate government spending took note, and voted accordingly. Unfortunately, Candidate Obama's promise to cut spending, like so many other campaign promises, evaporated in the light of day when he became president.

Obama impugned his predecessor, saying, "When George Bush came into office, our debt—national debt—was around $5 trillion. It's now over $10 trillion. We've almost doubled it … But actually I'm cutting more than I'm spending, so it will be a net spending cut."

Political spin aside, President Obama tripled the federal deficit in 2009 and presided over a national debt that was 30 percent higher in his second year than when he took over from President Bush.

We created more debt in two years under President Obama than we did in the first 200 years. Candidate Obama claimed he would be "cutting more than I'm spending, so it will be a net spending cut." The only things cut were the lines of trust with the American people.

Read More:

- *http://www.federalbudget.com*
- *http://www.foxnews.com/politics/2009/10/23/pub-obama-campaign-promises#ixzz1EpuK7OwR*

VIOLATING THE BASIC PRIVACY OF LAW-ABIDING AMERICANS

ATTACKING PRESIDENT BUSH, ONLY TO FOLLOW IN HIS FOOTSTEPS

WIRE TAP FLIP FLOP

"A federal judge ruled Wednesday that the National Security Agency's program of surveillance without warrants was illegal, rejecting the Obama administration's effort to keep shrouded in secrecy one of the most disputed counterterrorism policies of former President George W. Bush."

"For one thing, under an Obama presidency, Americans will be able to leave behind the era of George W. Bush, Dick Cheney and 'wiretaps without warrants.'"

"For one thing, under an Obama presidency, Americans will be able to leave behind the era of George W. Bush, Dick Cheney, and 'wiretaps without warrants.'"

—*Candidate Barack Obama*

As he worked to differentiate himself from the outgoing administration, Candidate Obama trained his sights on our government's practice of monitoring suspect communications without the traditional court order, a warrant.

Candidate Obama attacked the Bush administration for "illegal wiretaps" in the war on terror. Numerous times on the campaign trail he promised, emphatically, to end these wiretaps.

He made his position crystal clear while campaigning for the Democratic presidential nomination during a speech at Dartmouth College:

> For one thing, under an Obama presidency, Americans will be able to leave behind the era of George W. Bush, Dick Cheney and "wiretaps without warrants."

Candidate Obama scored significant political points, particularly with younger voters, during both the primary and the presidential campaign with his repeated promise to end wiretaps without warrants.

However, President Obama continues to break this promise to America, upholding the Bush administration's position that he so aggressively attacked while seeking election.

President Obama now finds himself defending the program he once condemned. A recent ruling from a federal judge declared that the wiretapping programs of both the Bush and Obama administrations were illegal.

The New York Times summarized the Obama wiretapping debacle:

> A federal judge ruled Wednesday that the National Security
> Agency's program of surveillance without warrants
> was illegal, rejecting the Obama administration's effort
> to keep shrouded in secrecy one of the most disputed
> counterterrorism policies of former President George W. Bush.

America had responded with hope to a promise from a seemingly sincere candidate, only to see him break his promise and pursue the very same agenda he once attacked and vigorously campaigned against.

If President Obama is now so far from Candidate Obama in 2008 on the issue of warrantless wiretapping, how can we believe President Obama's 2012 reelection promises?

Read More:

• *http://www.nytimes.com/2010/04/01/us/01nsa.html*

AN EAR FOR
THE SOUND OF PORK

INCREASING EARMARKS
EACH YEAR OF HIS PRESIDENCY

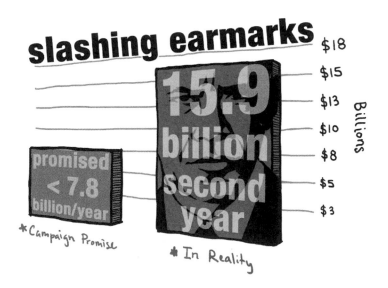

"[I will] slash earmarks by more than half when I am president."

—*Candidate Barack Obama*

Two months before the November 2008 presidential election, in a speech titled "The Change We Need in Washington," Candidate Obama aggressively attacked Republicans for increasing earmarks.

Obama promised in his speech to "slash earmarks by more than half" when he became president. Elsewhere on the campaign trail he promised to reduce earmarks to "less than $7.8 billion a year, the level they were at before 1994, when the Republicans took control of Congress."

Candidate Obama won votes and financial campaign contributions with these promises, only to break them when he became president. In keeping with his demonstrated tendency, President Obama disregarded both of his promises on earmarks.

Even with a House and Senate controlled by Democrats during his first two years of office, the president failed to keep either of his promises to reduce earmarks. Worse yet, the earmarks have increased each year he's been in office!

Despite Candidate Obama's promise to slash earmarks, once elected, he allowed them to exceed $15 billion in his first year and watched as earmarks increased to $15.9 billion (with 9,499 separate earmarks) in 2010.

Once again, voters picked a perceived winner but ended up the ultimate losers when it came to Obama's promises to reduce earmarks.

Read More:

- President Obama's "The Change We Need In Washington": www.BarackObama.com
- www.Taxpayers.Org
- http://obama.3cdn.net/0080cc578614b42284_2a0mvyxpz.pdf
- http://my.barackobama.com/page/community/post/amandascott/gGgySq

GAY MARRIAGE

"I favor legalizing same-sex marriages, and would fight efforts to prohibit such marriages."

> —Illinois Senate candidate Barack Obama, 1996

"I believe marriage is between a man and a woman. I am not in favor of gay marriage."

> —presidential candidate Barack Obama, 2008

"My opinion on gay marriage is evolving."

> —President Obama, seeking donations
> from gay rights activists, 2011

Shifting with the prevailing winds is a useful characteristic in a weathervane but a terrible quality in a leader. Unfortunately for America, Barack Obama seems to change his opinion on issues depending on what is most advantageous in the next election. Case in point: gay marriage.

As a Democratic candidate for the Illinois State Senate, Obama responded to a questionnaire from a Chicago publication for gays with a pledge of strong support for same-sex marriage. After all, supporting gay rights helps one's campaign in a Chicago Democratic primary.

However, when he became a candidate for president, Barack Obama decided he was "not in favor of gay marriage." Clearly, he and his pollster understood that supporting gay marriage could harm the prospects of a newly elected senator running for president in 2008.

Congressman Barney Frank (D-Massachusetts), one of Congress's most vocal gay-rights advocates, said on Obama's apparent flip-flops, "[Obama] was probably inclined to think that same-sex marriage was legitimate, but as a candidate for president in 2008 that would have been an unwise thing to say."

In 2012, as his reelection campaign works to raise $1 billion, Obama needs the support of every constituency, especially donations from the gay community.

Unfortunately for President Obama, critics in that community have been vocal in their disappointment, including Jared Polis, an openly gay congressman from Colorado. Polis recently stated that he "could understand why some in the gay or lesbian community would refuse to donate to Obama."

Curiously, the president is now reevaluating his position on gay marriage, saying his position is "evolving."

Within days of this and other, similar criticisms, the White House launched an official Web page for gays, lesbians, bisexuals, and transgender (GLBT) people: www.whitehouse.gov/lgbt.

Regardless of how one defines marriage, the bigger concern is: Do we want a president whose beliefs shift like the wind and, in the process, hangs key supporters out to dry?

Read More:

- http://www.whitehouse.gov/lgbt
- http://3.bp.blogspot.com/-6cS25-Ux1rc/TfuCruczA6l/AAAAAAAAGNA/8BxueWKmelg/s1600/Screen%2Bshot%2B2011-06-17%2Bat%2B11.35.58%2BAM.jpg
- http://www.nytimes.com/2011/06/19/us/politics/19marriage.html
- http://www.youtube.com/watch?v=73oZ_pe1MZ8
- http://www.cnn.com/ELECTION/2008/issues/issues.samesexmarriage.html
- http://blogs.abcnews.com/politicalradar/2008/11/obama-on-mtv-i.html
- http://thehill.com/blogs/blog-briefing-room/news/campaigns/civil-rights/47677-polis-i-can-understand-why-gay-donors-would-stop-obama-donations

NO INPUT NEEDED

RENEGING ON THE FIVE-DAYS-OF PUBLIC-COMMENT PROMISE

NON EMERGENCY BILL

5

OBAMACARE 48 HOUR VIOLATION

DAYS

"[I will not sign any] nonemergency bill without giving the American public an opportunity to review and comment on the White House website for five days."

—Candidate Barack Obama

The wheels of democracy turn slowly for a reason, allowing for debate and full disclosure of a law's effects on citizens. Playing on the growing distrust of elected officials in Washington and the "sticker shock" that accompanies countless spending bills, Candidate Obama promised a fresh approach to governance.

Candidate Obama repeatedly pledged not to sign any "nonemergency bill without giving the American public an opportunity to review and comment on the White House website for five days." President Obama has broken that promise so many times, in so many significant policy areas, that it's almost impossible to keep track.

However, some major breaches of the public confidence deserve special attention. The president's most famous violation of this promise occurred when he signed Obamacare into law within forty-eight hours of the House's final passage. Several members of Congress even publicly admitted that they hadn't had enough time to read the entire bill before voting on it.

The promise of openness that flowed so sweetly from Candidate Obama's lips became a mere afterthought for President Obama, as he quickly put pen to paper on numerous nonemergency bills (which fit the "nonemergency" category because they don't take effect for a full year). These included bills that impact personal credit and states' implementation of health care for children.

Once again, Candidate Obama painted a clear picture of a fresh, open approach to governance that was quickly obscured by actions in opposition to his promises.

Read More:

- http://www.nytimes.com/2010/03/24/health/policy/24health.html
- http://www.msnbc.msn.com/id/35986022/ns/politics-capitol_hill/
- http://thehill.com/blogs/blog-briefing-room/news/115749-sen-baucus-suggests-he-did-not-read-entire-health-bill
- http://www.politifact.com/truth-o-meter/promises/obameter/promise/234/allow-five-days-of-public-comment-before-signing-b/

NEVER GETTING BETTER

WHITE HOUSE NUMBERS
SHOW DEBT ONLY GOES ONE WAY

"What my budget does is ... by the middle of this decade our annual spending will match our annual revenues. We will not be adding more to the national debt."

—President Barack Obama

Regardless of their political affiliation, Americans are increasingly concerned with the massive deficit spending in Washington and the accompanying national debt load. Aware of the impact such an approach would have on their own personal budgets, Americans realize that such an approach to finance is not sustainable indefinitely.

In an attempt to quell those fears while presenting a budget laden with new spending, President Obama said, "What my budget does is ... by the middle of this decade our annual spending will match our annual revenues. We will not be adding more to the national debt."

Facts available through the White House website tell the truth: President Obama's budgets forecast both deficits and an increase in year-over-year national debt every year through 2020.

According to the president's own budgets, deficits for the next decade will be as follows:

Year	Debt	Year	Debt
2010	$1.293 trillion	2016	$649 billion
2011	$1.645 trillion	2017	$627 billion
2012	$1.101 trillion	2018	$619 billion
2013	$768 billion	2019	$681 billion
2014	$645 billion	2020	$735 billion
2015	$607 billion		

However, the annual deficits listed above are dwarfed by the debt burden accumulating on America. President Obama's budgets project public debt to the tune of:

Year	Debt	Year	Debt
2010	$9.019 trillion	2016	$15.064 trillion
2011	$10.856 trillion	2017	$15.795 trillion
2012	$11.881 trillion	2018	$16.513 trillion
2013	$12.784 trillion	2019	$17.284 trillion
2014	$13.562 trillion	2020	$18.103 trillion
2015	$14.301 trillion		

Some of the most pro-Obama economists have expressed concern that the president's projections are optimistic at best, so these forecasts could be much higher. Regardless, there's no debating that deficits, even going by President Obama's budget forecasts, will persist, and the national debt will increase—for every year from 2010 through 2020.

If numbers don't lie, then what (or who) does? With his claim that "by the middle of this decade our annual spending will match our annual revenues. We will not be adding more to the national debt," the answer is clearly: our president.

Read More:

- http://www.politifact.com/truth-o-meter/statements/2011/feb/15/barack-obama/barack-obama-says-white-house-budget-would-not-add/
- http://www.foxnews.com/politics/2009/10/23/pub-obama-campaign-promises#ixzz1EpuK7OwR

IMMIGRATION, SHIMMIGRATION!

CAMPAIGNED AS AN IMMIGRANT, ONLY TO IGNORE THEM ONCE ELECTED

immigration
reform

"But what I can guarantee is that we will have in the first year an immigration bill that I strongly support and that I'm promoting."

—Candidate Barack Obama

As the walking embodiment of the American melting pot, and covetous of votes from America's increasing minority population, Candidate Obama came out strongly in favor of comprehensive immigration reform.

He said, "I cannot guarantee that it is going to be in the first one hundred days. But what I can guarantee is that we will have in the first year an immigration bill that I strongly support and that I'm promoting. And I want to move that forward as quickly as possible."

Candidate Obama garnered millions of votes by promising to push comprehensive immigration reform in his first year and to level the "playing field for American workers" through immigration reform.

With the one-hundred-day mark come and gone many, many times, and the fourth year of his term proceeding apace, it is clear that President Obama will not be keeping Candidate Obama's promise of comprehensive immigration reform any time soon.

Candidate Obama displayed a campaign theme, but we couldn't see the theme in its entirety until we elected him president: As Candidate Obama he was willing to say whatever he thought we wanted to hear to gain our votes.

As president, Obama ignored what we said by voting for him —that we expect him to keep his word. Now, as he begins his campaign for reelection, he is resurrecting a broken promise from his last campaign: immigration reform, if only we'll reelect him.

President Obama's broken promise is more than failed political spin to the millions of immigrants living in the shadows; it moves them ever closer to genuine crisis.

Once again, broken promises litter the path of a man who offered such a compelling message of hope in exchange for votes.

Read More:

- *http://www.barackobama.com/issues/immigrationreform/index. php?source=BOnav*
- *http://www.politifact.com/truth-o-meter/statements/2008/sep/19/ barack-obama/limbaughs-not-a-mccain-spokesman/*
- *http://voices.washingtonpost.com/44/2008/09/obama-invokes-rush-limbaugh-in.html*
- *http://www.cbsnews.com/8301-503544_162-5097178-503544.html*
- *http://www.ontheissues.org/barack_obama.htm*

LOBBY FOR A JOB?

LOBBYISTS REGULATING THEIR FORMER EMPLOYERS

NO MORE LOBBYISTS...

EXCEPT FOR THESE

"When you walk into my administration, you will not be able to work on regulations or contracts directly related to your former employer for two years."

—Candidate Barack Obama

For Americans disgusted by the role of special interests in government, Candidate Obama's promises to end the impact of lobbyists at the highest levels in Washington were encouraging indeed.

Unfortunately, as he has in so many other areas, President Obama not only broke that promise right after being elected, but continues breaking it to this day.

Immediately upon being elected president, his nominee for deputy defense secretary was William Lynn, who just months earlier had been a registered lobbyist for the behemoth defense contractor Raytheon.

Lynn is one of a large group of former lobbyists in President Obama's inner circle. According to one source, "More than forty former lobbyists work in senior positions in the Obama administration, including three cabinet secretaries and the CIA director."

If a candidate promises that people in his administration "will not be able to work on regulations or contracts directly related to [their] former employer for two years," yet recent lobbyists appear in his cabinet overseeing their former industries once he is elected, you have to ask if that person is a liar. And the answer inevitably is yes.

Despite Candidate Obama's promises to the contrary, the White House and executive offices are riddled with former lobbyists who now directly impact the companies and industries they lobbied less than two years earlier.

Sadly, special interests continue to steer the ship of state in Washington, DC. Even more sadly, our president continues to prove that we traded our votes for his lies and our hard-earned money for his special interests.

Read More:

- http://washingtonexaminer.com/politics/obama-makes-mockery-his-own-lobbyist-ban#ixzz1Gra1EoYc
- http://www.foxnews.com/politics/2009/10/23/pub-obama-campaign-promises#ixzz1EptuGWj9

READY, FIRE, AIM

IGNORING THE CONSTITUTION AND HIS OWN WORDS

"The president does not have the power under the Constitution to unilaterally authorize a military attack in a situation that does not involve stopping an actual or imminent threat to the nation."

—Candidate Barack Obama

Although George W. Bush was not in the 2008 presidential race, Candidate Obama campaigned as if he were, repeatedly attacking him for the nation's involvement in Iraq and Afghanistan. One frequent argument from the candidate, a professor of constitutional law, was this: "The president does not have the power under the Constitution to unilaterally authorize a military attack in a situation that does not involve stopping an actual or imminent threat to the nation."

In an increasingly war-weary nation, Candidate Obama relied on his predecessor's abuse of executive power to position himself as an enlightened leader driven by the Constitution.

Obama's fascination with constitutional limits on presidential power was obliterated by his unilateral decision to attack targets that were not imminent threats to the United States.

In early 2011, with the Middle East in upheaval and political protests breaking out in major urban centers throughout the Muslim world, President Obama remained oddly detached from the situation.

That is, until he announced on March 19th that U.S. forces had begun bombing Libya—with none of the congressional consent Candidate Obama had pledged to obtain as a precondition. President Obama "unilaterally authorized a military attack" in a situation that "did not involve stopping an actual or imminent threat" to America.

Candidate Obama lied or President Obama broke the law. Either instance is telling as a lack of character and credibility.

President Obama's indifference to constitutional law and his willingness to authorize a unilateral military action are beyond troubling. For hundreds in Libya, both military and civilian, his disregard for the law and failure to keep his word have proved deadly.

Read More:

- http://www.boston.com/news/politics/2008/specials/CandidateQA/ObamaQA/
- http://news.yahoo.com/s/ap/lt_libya_obama

GOOD ENOUGH FOR THE LITTLE PEOPLE

EVERY AMERICAN WILL HAVE THE SAME HEALTH CARE AS CONGRESS ... OR NOT

SAME HEALTH CARE?

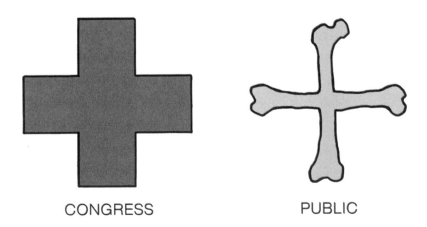

CONGRESS   PUBLIC

"[Americans will have] the same choice of private health insurance that members of Congress get for themselves."

—President Barack Obama

Candidate Obama often cited the need for fairness in health insurance, claiming his plan, Obamacare, would give Americans the same high-quality health insurance that Congress and the president receive.

Once elected president, he promised, Obamacare would give us all "the same choice of private health insurance that members of Congress get for themselves."

President Obama pledged that his health insurance would "be affecting every American family" and that every American would be "part of a big pool, just like federal employees are part of a big pool. They'll have the same choice of private health insurance that members of Congress get for themselves."

Obamacare became law when the president hurriedly signed it within forty-eight hours of its passage, breaking another of his promises: to allow five days of public input before signing a bill into law. Obama signed it after allowing members of Congress to exempt themselves from having to join Obamacare, the insurance mandate Obama forced on the public.

Obama signed Obamacare—which he had promised would give the average Joe the same insurance "that members of Congress get for themselves"—after Congress voted to exempt themselves from it.

Obviously, the average American does not have "the same

choice of private health insurance that members of Congress get for themselves."

President Obama broke this promise to America by signing health insurance legislation that created a system so bad that the president and Congress are exempt from participating.

If Obamacare is so bad, then why is the president forcing the rest of us into it? Perhaps for the same reason the public school system is not good enough for Obama's children (see "Won't Vouch for Vouchers").

Candidate Obama presented a façade of a humble man willing to roll up his sleeves and rub elbows with average Americans. President Obama presents a pattern of entitlement and elitism: one set of rules for himself and the political elites and another for the rest of us.

Read More:

- *http://www.barackobama.com/pdf/issues/HealthCareFullPlan.pdf*
- *http://www.washingtontimes.com/news/2010/mar/23/obamacare-for-everyone-but-obama/*

REASON 11

I AM NOT A CROOK...

TWISTING THE FACTS ON
HIS CAMPAIGN CONTRIBUTIONS

"I'm Barack Obama...I don't take money from oil companies"

"I'm Barack Obama ... I don't take money from oil companies or Washington lobbyists, and I won't let them block change anymore."

—Candidate Barack Obama

There are certain segments of American society that resent big corporations, regardless of what they produce or whom they employ. As a result, a candidate can seek outsider status by attacking the establishment, which includes major corporations.

Candidate Obama proclaimed himself an outsider by running commercials in which he said, "I'm Barack Obama. I don't take money from oil companies or Washington lobbyists, and I won't let them block change anymore."

At worst this claim was a lie. At best it was a gross mischaracterization of the truth, achieved through a delicate parsing of words intended to deceive us, the voters.

Until a January 2010, U.S. Supreme Court ruling on corporate campaign contributions, it was illegal to take money from oil companies. So, in fact, none of the candidates took money from oil companies during the last election.

With such nuanced phrasing, Candidate Obama implied that he maintained a higher degree of ethical purity than his opponents. Obama misled voters into believing that his campaign did not receive campaign contributions from oil companies, even as he accepted donations from oil and gas company executives, their spouses, and their employees, to the tune of over $213,000.

In addition, Barack Obama's campaign website listed two oil executives as top fundraisers, each of whom "bundled" between fifty thousand dollars and one hundred thousand dollars for him.

Candidate Obama garnered significant electoral support by attacking people and industries for political gain. When he cleverly claimed, "I don't take money from oil companies," he showed a willingness to shade the truth, perhaps even to lie, to get our votes.

Candidate Obama's clever proclamations about not taking money from oil companies only supported his political interests, not the interests of the people he was elected to serve.

Read More:

• *http://www.factcheck.org/elections-2008/obamas_oil_spill.html*

LOOK AMERICA, NO HANDS!

WHEN YOU CAN'T BLAME BUSH ANYMORE, DENY IT EVER HAPPENED

"Tax Increases?"

"YES WE CAN!"

"I didn't raise taxes once. I lowered taxes over the last two years."

—President Barack Obama (2/6/11)

The phrase "I didn't raise taxes" seems crystal clear and certainly, when said by the president, everyone could be confident of its meaning. However, this statement must mean something different to President Barack Obama.

Americans are aware when the cost of something goes up. When something costs more due to a change in taxes, Americans call this a tax increase. Seems simple enough.

Americans using health savings accounts saw increased taxes on their withdrawals: Those who smoke coughed up sixty-two cents more a pack, and tanning bed users found their financial hides tanned as well. President Obama also increased taxes on "Cadillac" health insurance plans, unless these plans were for union members.

All of these tax increases occurred in spite of promises made repeatedly by Candidate Obama that families making less than $250,000 "will not see any of your taxes increase one single dime."

Then there is the tax by another name: Obamacare. Under Obamacare, if you do not want to pay for health insurance, too bad. The government is going to force you to spend money on it. In any other world this would be considered a tax increase, a big one, but in Obama-land it means: "I lowered taxes over the last two years."

In an ironic twist, the Obama administration denied that Obamacare was a tax while they were forcing the legislation through Congress. Now the president's lawyers are arguing that his namesake law *is* a tax in an effort to defend its constitutionality in the courts. If Obamacare is a tax, then Congress may have the constitutional authority to enact the law, which is why the president's team has flip-flopped on labeling it a tax. If it's a mandate, then there's a strong constitutional question whether it's legal. What's important for our purposes is Obama's lack of honesty concerning his increasing taxes.

All of these tax increases (and others) occurred during the "last two years" President Obama referred to on February 6, 2011. A revelation that should give all voters pause.

President Obama had the audacity to go on national television during the Super Bowl two years into his term, look Americans in the eye, and claim that he "didn't raise taxes once."

In one sense he was right: he raised them several times.

Read More:

- *http://cnsnews.com/news/article/obama-s-claim-he-did-not-raise-taxes-rej*
- *http://www.youtube.com/watch?v=t6HyXCHndmk 5:35 into the interview.*
- *http://www.heritage.org/research/reports/2011/01/obamacare-and-new-taxes-destroying-jobs-and-the-economy*
- *http://www.realclearpolitics.com/news/ap/politics/2009/Apr/01/ promises__promises__obama_tax_pledge_up_in_smoke.html*

I WAS AGAINST THE MANDATE; BEFORE I WAS FOR THE MANDATE

"THE DIFFERENCE BETWEEN HILLARY'S PLAN AND MINE IS, HERS IS A MANDATE, MINE IS NOT"... UNTIL I BECOME PRESIDENT

"IF YOU'VE GOT A HEALTHCARE PLAN THAT YOU LIKE, YOU CAN KEEP IT... THERE'S NO MANDATE INVOLVED"

THE OBAMACARE MANDATE CREATES A TAX PENALTY FOR UNINSURED AMERICANS

"If you've got a health care plan that you like, you can keep it ... there's no mandate involved."

—Candidate Barack Obama

Candidate Obama's pointed attacks on the campaign trail were not reserved for his Republican foes. Finding himself neck and neck with Hillary Clinton in the Democratic primaries, he went on the offensive, taking aim at her proposed health insurance plan.

Candidate Obama repeatedly attacked Clinton for mandating health insurance and contrasted his own plan by saying, "If you've got a health care plan that you like, you can keep it ... there's no mandate involved."

The tide that swept Obama into office no doubt included votes from those he convinced would not be forced to buy health insurance nor endure mandates for it.

Using the Democratic majorities in both houses of Congress, President Obama methodically, relentlessly forced Obamacare into law, despite protests from legislators, health care practitioners and countless citizen groups. Their fears were realized when they found, buried in the endless pages of the bill, a section that fines people for not buying health insurance, the textbook definition of a mandate.

The Obamacare mandate creates a tax penalty for uninsured Americans:

> Those without coverage could eventually (by 2016) pay a tax penalty greater than $695 per year up to a maximum

of three times that amount ($2,085) per family or
2.5 percent of household income. The penalty will be
phased in. After 2016, the penalty will be increased
annually by the cost-of-living adjustment.

Though many in America feel deceived by President Obama's
health insurance mandate—the one that Candidate Obama
swore would *not* be a mandate—perhaps no one in America has
been more harmed by this deceit than Hillary Clinton.

Had Mr. Obama been honest and willing to be judged by his true
plans, it's possible that Hillary Clinton would be president.

Instead, America has a president who will say one thing to get
elected and then do another once in power—the worst kind
of politician.

Read More:

• http://www.politifact.com/virginia/statements/2010/dec/20/bob-
marshall/del-bob-marshall-says-violators-obama-health-care-/
• http://www.foxnews.com/politics/2009/10/23/pub-obama-campaign-
promises#ixzz1EpuZVBrV

SICK PEOPLE
SHOULD PAY MORE

SUCKING UP TO PHARMACY LOBBYISTS
AND BREAKING HIS PROMISE

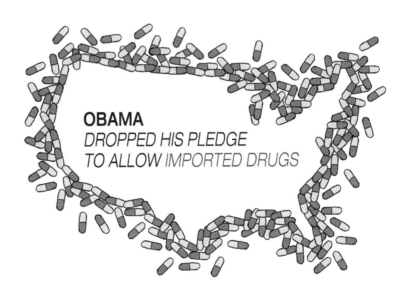

OBAMA
*DROPPED HIS PLEDGE
TO ALLOW IMPORTED DRUGS*

*"Allow Americans to buy their medicines from other
developed countries if the drugs are safe and prices are
lower outside the U.S."*

—Candidate Barack Obama

On the campaign trail Candidate Obama managed to combine his affection for bashing large corporations and playing on the fears of the electorate by attacking drug companies and the profits they make. Knowing that many Americans, including a number of senior citizens, were already visiting Canada to buy less expensive prescription drugs (in violation of U.S. law), he seized this opportunity.

A key element of Candidate Obama's health insurance reform proposal was to "allow Americans to buy their medicines from other developed countries if the drugs are safe and prices are lower outside the U.S."

Along with Candidate Obama's many other promises of change, this popular position helped him win the presidency. Like so many of his promises, President Obama broke this one by steering a course in the opposite direction, cutting a deal with the drug industry's main lobbyist, former congressman Billy Tauzin.

During a closed-door meeting with Tauzin, President Obama not only agreed to kill an initiative to get better prescription prices through Medicare, but also dropped his pledge to allow Americans to buy cheaper imported drugs from Canada or Europe.

Campaigning on a pledge to "allow Americans to buy their medicines from other developed countries if the drugs are safe and prices are lower outside the U.S." and then completely reversing course is not just campaigning. It's lying.

Another sad dose of reality about Obama's intentions.

Read More:

- http://www.barackobama.com/pdf/issues/HealthCareFullPlan.pdf
- http://www.latimes.com/features/health/la-na-healthcare-pharma4-2009aug04,0,3660985.story
- http://www.politifact.com/truth-o-meter/promises/obameter/promise/71/allow-imported-prescription-drugs/

ON A FIXED INCOME? PAY ME!

AND TO THE GREATEST GENERATION: BROKEN PROMISE ON TAX RELIEF

NO TAX BREAKS FOR SENIORS

"[I will] eliminate all income taxation of seniors making less than fifty thousand dollars per year."

—*Candidate Barack Obama*

Candidate Obama's words struck a chord with senior citizens, especially his promise to:

> Eliminate all income taxation of seniors making less than fifty thousand dollars per year. This will eliminate taxes for seven million seniors—saving them an average of fourteen hundred dollars a year—and will also mean that twenty-seven million seniors will not need to file an income tax return at all.

Many political analysts agree that Candidate Obama received a large segment of the senior citizen vote, thanks in part to this promise to eliminate taxes for seniors making less than fifty thousand a year.

Those senior citizens—many of whom survived wars and worked to rebuild the nation afterward—have been abandoned by a young man with a silver tongue and a tin ear. Three years after his election President Obama has yet to keep Candidate Obama's promise to low-income seniors.

None of the budgets President Obama released for 2009, 2010, or 2011 kept Candidate Obama's promise. Instead, those taxes continue.

This tragic disregard for the Greatest Generation demonstrates a mercenary emphasis on getting votes and a callous disregard for the truth—hardly appropriate behavior for the commander in chief.

Read More:

- http://www.barackobama.com/pdf/taxes/Factsheet_Tax_Plan_FINAL.pdf
- http://online.wsj.com/article/SB10001424052748703652104576122520508633078.html

EXPENSIVE GASOLINE: GOVERNMENT'S PROFITS GOOD; OIL COMPANIES' PROFITS BAD

OBAMA VOTED FOR A FIFTY-SEVEN CENT PER GALLON GAS TAX, THEN ATTACKED OIL COMPANIES FOR EXPENSIVE GASOLINE

"There is no magic formula to driving gas prices down."

—President Barack Obama

The average combined federal and state excise tax on a gallon of gasoline sold in America is forty cents. The average profit on a gallon of gasoline for Exxon Mobil is eight cents. Yet Barack Obama (as Senator Obama, Candidate Obama, and President Obama) has repeatedly maligned oil companies for their profits while refusing to consider lowering gas taxes.

When average Americans fill up a fifteen-gallon tank they're paying six dollars in federal and state taxes, about three hundred dollars a year.

Drivers face even higher gasoline taxes in places like Chicago, Illinois, President Obama's hometown where the combined federal and state tax is 57.4 cents per gallon. They end up paying over $9.20 in taxes on every fill-up (or about $450 a year).

President Obama laments high gasoline prices as a threat to the nation's economy but refuses to consider reducing the amount of tax we pay per gallon. Instead, he laughingly tells us, "If you're complaining about the price of gas, and you're only getting eight miles a gallon ... you might want to think about a trade-in."

Although he claims "there's no magic formula to driving gas prices down," Obama should understand that if you reduce the supply of oil, you will increase the cost of gasoline. Surely a lawyer from Harvard understands this basic economic tenet of supply and demand.

However, Obama has repeatedly reduced domestic oil production. Among other policies that have resulted in a reduced domestic oil supply, he has:

- canceled seventy-seven leases for oil and gas drilling in Utah;

- instituted two outright drilling bans in the Gulf of Mexico; and

- refused to issue any new drilling permits in the Gulf of Mexico (The Energy Information Administration estimates this will cut domestic offshore oil production by 13 percent).

Obama has a long history of complaining about gasoline prices while increasing gasoline taxes. When he was an Illinois state senator, that state had one of the country's highest gasoline taxes. Senator Obama had an opportunity to permanently lower gas prices in his state, but he voted against doing so.

This opportunity arose due to skyrocketing gasoline prices and overtaxation. The Illinois legislature temporarily repealed its gasoline sales tax of 5 percent per gallon. This was a much-needed financial relief for all drivers, especially low-income ones for whom gasoline is a major monthly expense. It was such good policy that a bill was introduced in the Illinois legislature to make the tax repeal permanent.

When the bill came up for a vote, state senator Obama voted against it.

It is hypocritical for Candidate Obama, and now President Obama, to lament the high price of gasoline when state senator Obama refused to reduce it for his constituents.

Such hypocrisy raises the question: Is President Obama's priority the fiscal freedom of America's citizens or the defense of high taxes that fuel ever-increasing government spending?

Read More:

- http://www.illinoisgasprices.com/tax_info.aspx
- http://www.taxfoundation.org/news/show/245.html
- senate.gov/~hutchison/speec111.htm
- http://washingtonexaminer.com/blogs/beltway-confidential/2011/04/obama-voter-gas-prices-you-might-want-think-about-trade#ixzz1NT9qfTx8

DID I SAY THAT?

KEEPING THE GUANTÁNAMO BAY DETENTION FACILITY OPEN

"Guantánamo has become a recruiting tool for our enemies ... The first step to reclaiming America's standing in the world has to be closing this facility."

—Candidate Barack Obama

With increasing allegations from news and civil rights organizations that the United States was mistreating detainees suspected of terrorism, public sentiment grew in opposition to the Cuban detainment facility. In response, Candidate Obama went to great lengths to question the necessity of the Guantánamo Bay facility and belittled President Bush and other Republicans on the campaign trail for their opposing stance.

Candidate Obama stated, "Guantánamo has become a recruiting tool for our enemies ... The first step to reclaiming America's standing in the world has to be closing this facility."

Despite votes from those who took him at his word, President Obama seemingly forgot his pledge to shut down the facility. Obama's presidency has a theme brewing: a promise from Candidate Obama, a broken promise from President Obama.

Days after taking office, President Obama drew America's attention to an executive order he had signed, which states:

> The detention facilities at Guantánamo for individuals covered by this order shall be closed as soon as practicable, and no later than one year from the date of this order (January 22, 2009).

Three years after Candidate Obama became President Obama, 172 detainees remained at Guantánamo Bay, Cuba, and he is now allowing military trials to resume there.

This appears to be yet another example of Candidate Obama telling voters what they want to hear and then presenting himself as a liar as president, both to voters and the world.

Americans must ask themselves whether Candidate Obama was honest when he made that promise or if he is no longer committed to restoring "America's standing in the world."

Perhaps President Obama should focus on his standing in the world, and on his ability to keep his word. Rather than another broken promise about closing Guantánamo, maybe he should simply close his mouth when he knows he's about to make another promise he doesn't intend to keep.

Read More:

- http://www.nytimes.com/2011/03/08/world/americas/08guantanamo.html
- http://www.nationalreview.com/campaign-spot/4701/long-post-complete-list-obama-statement-expiration-dates
- http://www.politifact.com/truth-o-meter/promises/obameter/promise/177/close-the-guantanamo-bay-detention-center/

WHERE THERE IS GLORY, THERE I SHALL BE

A THREE-YEAR-OLD IS CONCEIVED ON THE STREETS OF SELMA

SELMA ALABAMA

OBAMA: AGE 3

"[I]t might not be possible for us to get together and have a child, but something is stirring across the country because of what happened in Selma, Alabama, because some folks are willing to march across the bridge. And so they got together and Barack Obama, Jr. was born. So don't tell me I don't have a claim on Selma, Alabama."

—Candidate Barack Obama

In an effort to associate himself with the landmark civil rights movement in Alabama, Candidate Obama committed a shameless display of political grandstanding and credited the famous Selma civil rights march for his very existence on Earth.

Obama claims his biracial parents (his mother was Caucasian and his father was black and from Kenya) had an epiphany as they reflected on the bravery of the Selma protesters on what is known as Bloody Sunday:

> They looked at each other and they decided, "We know that in the world, as it has been, it might not be possible for us to get together and have a child, but something is stirring across the country because of what happened in Selma, Alabama, because some folks are willing to march across the bridge." And so they got together and Barack Obama Jr. was born. So don't tell me I don't have a claim on Selma, Alabama!

This account certainly makes for good political theater, but it describes an impossible scenario. President Obama was born in 1961, more than three years before civil rights protesters took to Selma's streets.

When he was called out for his misleading anecdote, Candidate Obama backtracked, saying he meant to credit the entire civil rights movement for his parents' union, not just the Bloody Sunday marchers. His backtracking is more than curious since he used the past tense in reference to Selma's freedom march when describing his parents' feelings about having a child together.

Candidate Obama told this story to a crowd and used the past tense throughout: "what happened in Selma" and "so they got together and Barack Obama, Jr. was born." During the campaign Obama showed a willingness to tell voters what they wanted to hear. In this instance, he was likely doing the same— only this time history proved him a liar rather than his actions after he was elected.

In a country where citizens cherish their hard-won freedoms and opportunities, every American can feel proud of the Selma marchers' bravery and remorse for the racism that made their march necessary.

However, manufacturing a false personal history to claim involvement in an important historical moment is an affront to those civil rights activists and should outrage every American.

Read More:

* http://voices.washingtonpost.com/factchecker/2008/03/obamas_camelot_connection.html

THE AUDACITY OF HOPE OR *THE AUDACITY OF HYPOCRISY?*

DEMOCRATIC SENATOR ON OBAMA: HE "FAILED TO LEAD THIS DEBATE OR OFFER A SERIOUS PROPOSAL FOR SPENDING AND CUTS."

"[This country must] require a government that lives within its means."

—President Barack Obama

Of all of Barack Obama's strengths, his ability as an orator is prodigious. His power to rivet listeners with perfectly chosen words and stories of human toil and trial has served him well in his ascent. Unfortunately, Obama often fails to follow through on his words.

On February 26, 2011, as the global economy continued to sputter, President Obama addressed the nation and struck a chord of fiscal responsibility. He said, "We can outeducate, outinnovate and outbuild the rest of the world. Doing that will require a government that lives within its means."

Less than two weeks after making the case for tightening the country's budget belt, President Obama encouraged Congress to raise the federal debt limit so that he could spend more. The president's request for a higher limit is even more unsettling given the fact that his budget already projects more than $1 trillion in deficit spending in 2012.

Elected leaders from both parties have spoken out about the president's failure to offer spending cuts in the face of a trillion-dollar-plus deficit. Freshman senator Joe Manchin (Democrat—West Virginia) took President Obama to task on the budget and spending cuts, saying he "failed to lead this debate or offer a serious proposal for spending and cuts."

Regardless of one's political affiliation, it's offensive that the president had the audacity to goad America to "live within its means" one day and two weeks later pressure Congress to raise the debt limit and allow more government spending.

When they read or heard about his book *The Audacity of Hope,* many placed the emphasis on the word "hope." In fact, President Obama has been the embodiment of audacity, bordering on hypocrisy.

Americans have a right to expect—if not insist—that our elected leaders not only do what they say but also take their own advice.

Read More:

- *http://www.whitehouse.gov/sites/default/files/omb/budget/fy2012/assets/tables.pdf*
- *http://content.usatoday.com/communities/onpolitics/post/2011/03/joe-manchin-barack-obama-budget-/1?loc=interstitialskip*

THE FACTS ARE UNDENIABLE ...
UNLESS I DENY THEM

CONVENIENTLY IGNORING GENOCIDE

"I WILL RECOGNIZE ARMENIAN GENO CIDE"

"[It is] my firmly held conviction that the Armenian Genocide is not an allegation, a personal opinion, or a point of view, but rather a widely documented fact supported by an overwhelming body of evidence. The facts are undeniable."

—Candidate Barack Obama

In seeking the office of president, Candidate Obama launched attacks against his opponents from every direction imaginable. One instance concerns the nation of Turkey circa 1915 when there was a wholesale slaughter of Armenians at the hands of the Turks. On the campaign trail, Obama promised he would "recognize the Armenian Genocide" and attacked Republicans on that issue.

He said:

> I shared with Secretary Rice my firmly held conviction that the Armenian Genocide is not an allegation, a personal opinion, or a point of view, but rather a widely documented fact supported by an overwhelming body of historical evidence. The facts are undeniable. An official policy that calls on diplomats to distort the historical facts is an untenable policy.

Once elected, President Obama was given an opportunity to accelerate the sort of healing process he so loves. Yet he deliberately broke his promise and refused to recognize the slaughter of Armenians as genocide.

On March 5, 2010, just two years after President Obama took office, a golden opportunity presented itself in the form of a 23 to 22 vote by the House Foreign Affairs Committee on the aptly named Armenian Genocide Resolution. It officially recognized as genocide the 1.5 million deaths that occurred between 1915 and 1923 at the hands of the Ottoman Empire.

Expecting the president to make good on his support for the Armenian Genocide Resolution, onlookers were startled when his secretary of state, Hillary Clinton, said: "The Obama Administration strongly opposes the resolution that was passed by only one vote by the House committee and will work very hard to make sure it does not go to the House floor."

How is it that a man who once stated, "An official policy that calls on diplomats to distort the historical facts is an untenable policy" could do such a complete about-face?

Apparently, denying what was previously found undeniable and "a widely held fact supported by an overwhelming body of historical evidence" is appropriate for this president. Perhaps President Obama was really telling Congress to "do as I say, not as I do."

Armenian genocide: another example of Candidate Obama saying one thing and President Obama doing another.

Read More:

- *http://www.barackobama.com/2008/01/19/*
- *http://www.aysor.am/en/news/2011/04/24/genocide-armenia-us/*
- *http://www.politifact.com/truth-o-meter/promises/obameter/ promise/511/recognize-armenian-genocide/*

WHEN FREE SPEECH IS EMBARRASSING, SEND IN THE COPS

WIKILEAKS AND THE RULE OF LAW

PROSECUTING WHAT THE PRESIDENT IS ENCOURAGING

"The Internet and traditional media outlets are critical in facilitating communication by and between Americans and citizens of the world. As president, Barack Obama will ensure that these critical communications pathways remain accessible to all Americans and reflect the diversity of our nation. By doing so, this policy will enable Americans to discuss and debate more actively the key issues that affect our lives and will give citizens greater autonomy to determine where the truth lies."

—*Candidate Barack Obama's website*

As part of President Obama's professed desire to encourage freedom around the world, Secretary of State Hillary Clinton said the Obama administration spent:

> $25 million this year on initiatives designed to protect bloggers and help them get around curbs like the Great Firewall of China, the gagging of social media sites in Iran, Cuba, Syria, Vietnam, and Myanmar as well as Egypt's recent unsuccessful attempt to thwart anti-government protests by simply pulling the plug on online communication.

Upon announcing the $25-million expenditure to help ensure Internet speech globally, Clinton added:

> Leaders worldwide have a choice to make. They can let the Internet in their countries flourish, and take the risk that the freedoms it enables will lead to a greater demand for political rights. Or they can constrict the Internet, choke the freedoms it naturally sustains, and risk losing all the economic and social benefits that come from a networked society.

Given their professed passion for free expression on the Internet, is it not ironic that President Obama's Justice Department is seeking to prosecute WikiLeaks founder Julian Assange? It's hypocritical. Assange gained worldwide notoriety when the site he founded disseminated reams of classified information, including U.S. diplomatic cables.

Despite the fact that Mr. Assange is not a U.S. citizen, and neither traveled to the United States to receive this classified information nor stole it, he is a target of U.S. prosecutors. While the U.S. serviceman who delivered this information to WikiLeaks is incarcerated, the Obama administration is aggressively seeking to prosecute Assange for doing the very thing that it is spending $25 million in taxpayer money to encourage in other nations.

Vice President Joseph Biden went so far as to call Assange a "hi-tech terrorist" for doing the very thing the Obama Administration encouraged: disseminating information about a government while that government tries to block it.

Candidate Obama's website claimed:

> The Internet and traditional media outlets are critical in facilitating communication by and between Americans and citizens of the world. As president, Barack Obama will ensure that these critical communications pathways remain accessible to all Americans and reflect the diversity of our nation. By doing so, this policy will enable Americans to discuss and debate more actively the key issues that affect our lives and will give citizens greater autonomy to determine where the truth lies.

President Obama seeks the prosecution of Julian Assange for communicating with Americans about our government for allowing our "citizens greater autonomy to determine where the truth lies" concerning our government.

If Julian Assange and WikiLeaks are "hi-tech terrorists" for doing the very thing that America is spending $25 million to have done to other governments, then what does that make President Obama?

The word hypocrite comes to mind.

Read More:

- *http://obama.3cdn.net/780e0e91ccb6cdbf6e_6udymvin7.pdf*
- *http://www.time.com/time/nation/article/0,8599,2058340,00.html#ixzz1HBtaqJP6*
- *http://www.dailykos.com/story/2011/02/16/945422/-Does-Secretary-Clinton-Have-a-Double-Standard-on-Internet-Freedom*
- *http://www.nytimes.com/2011/06/12/world/12internet.html*

NO MORTGAGE ON WHITE HOUSE, NOT MY PROBLEM.

/////

BROKEN PROMISE OF 10 PERCENT MORTGAGE CREDIT FOR EVERY HOMEOWNER

10% UNIVERSAL MORTGAGE CREDIT

FORGOTTEN

"[My administration will be] creating a 10 percent universal mortgage credit that gives tax relief to all Americans who have a home mortgage."

—Candidate Barack Obama

Candidate Obama presented himself as a champion of the middle class, rolling up his sleeves for factory photo ops and promising a raft of help to working Americans. He dangled a giant carrot in front of homeowners in the form of a "10 percent universal mortgage credit that gives tax relief to all Americans who have a home mortgage."

Obama told voters:

> Many middle-class Americans do not receive the existing mortgage interest tax deduction because they do not itemize their taxes ... Obama and Biden will ensure that middle-class Americans get the financial assistance they need to purchase or keep their own home by creating a 10 percent universal mortgage credit that gives tax relief to all Americans who have a home mortgage.

Candidate Obama was very deliberate in selling his 10 percent mortgage credit and detailed in how it would help families struggling to make their mortgage payments.

With those middle-class homeowner votes in hand, President Obama shifted his mailing address to 1600 Pennsylvania Avenue and forgot about his promise to them. In doing so, Obama exposed yet another crack in his foundation.

Read More:

- *http://www.usatoday.com/news/politics/election2008/2007-09-18-obama-tax-plan_N.htmhttp://change.gov/agenda/economy_agenda/*
- *http://www.barackobama.com/pdf/issues/UrbanFactSheet.pdf*

WON'T VOUCH FOR VOUCHERS

POOR CHILDREN IN BAD SCHOOLS JUST NEED RICH PARENTS

NO MORE
SCHOOL CHOICE

"A U.S. Senator can get his kid into a terrific public school. That's not the question. The question is whether or not ordinary parents, who can't work the system, are able to get their kids into a decent school, and that's what I need to fight for and will fight for as president."

—Candidate Barack Obama

Americans pay taxes to fund our public school systems. But only those wealthy enough to afford private tuition can send their children to the school of their choice. Longstanding (if misguided) laws trap families in the public school district where they reside, even when those schools fail to provide an adequate education.

President Obama is one of the fortunate few who can send his children to the school of his choice, in his case a private school. Yet the president opposes efforts to extend that choice to parents with lesser financial means than his own.

School choice advocates were astonished when the candidate who had spoken so passionately about the importance of education in improving one's lot in life killed a program in Washington, DC that gave low-income parents tuition vouchers of up to seventy-five hundred dollars a year to send their children to private schools. Surely this was not the hope those voters had believed in.

Candidate Obama said he'd fight as president for parents to be able to "get their kids in a decent school." Many low-income families in Washington, DC had the means to send their kids to decent schools through this program until Obama was elected president.

These families had their children in those schools because they were given tuition vouchers: Their children could attend private schools instead of being forced into some of the nation's worst-performing public ones. Unfortunately for these parents, the candidate who promised to fight to ensure that ordinary "parents … are able to get their kids into decent schools" became the president who ensured that these parents' hope of a decent education for their children was destroyed.

Most school-choice opponents claim such programs divert money from public schools. However, these programs divert not only money but also the expense of educating the child. The political reality is that public school unions (Democrats' single biggest campaign donors) don't want the competition, nor do public school administrations want their tax-dollar monopolies threatened.

It is hypocritical that a former inner-city community organizer, who now occupies the most powerful office in the world, sends his children to private schools because he can afford to while blocking that right for poor families who can't.

President Obama's pattern of hypocrisy continues; even the public schools would give Obama an F for failing.

Read More:

- http://educationtaxcredits.com/2008/07/barack-obama-opposes-vouchers.html
- http://www.bloomberg.com/apps/news?sid=aagk5hr_wShs&pid=newsarchive

WE'RE IN THE MONEY; IT DON'T LOOK SUNNY

KEEPING FEDERAL CONTRACTS IN THE SHADOWS AND AMONG FRIENDS

LIE

"FEDERAL CONTRACTS OVER $25,000 ARE COMPETITIVELY BID"

"[If elected president I will] ensure that federal contracts over twenty-five thousand dollars are competitively bid."

—Candidate Barack Obama

Corruption has afflicted governments since their beginnings, but citizens in an open, democratic society want to live under leadership that adheres to the highest ethical standards.

In particular, the apportionment of tax dollars in seemingly shady ways sets off alarm bells for voters and puts them on the alert for a candidate who promises the highest ethical standards. Enter Candidate Obama.

On the campaign trail Candidate Obama took aim at government appropriations and contracting, raising doubts about the fairness of contracts awarded without a suitable bidding process.

His simple stance? A pledge to "ensure that federal contracts over twenty-five thousand dollars are competitively bid."

Candidate Obama promised to "increase the efficiency of government programs through better use of technology, stronger management that demands accountability, and by leveraging the government's high-volume purchasing power to get lower prices." President Obama didn't lower the cost of government for the taxpayers: The only thing that was lowered was citizens' regard for his honesty, thanks to deals like the one awarded to a major Democratic donor.

On January 4, 2010, the U.S. Agency for International Development awarded a $24,673,427 no-bid contract to Checchi and Company Consulting, Inc., a Washington-based firm owned by economist and Democratic donor Vincent V. Checchi.

Checchi and Company was hired to "train the next generation of legal professionals" and "develop the capacity of Afghanistan's justice system to be accessible, reliable, and fair"; their contract served to highlight the fact that President Obama's bid process was not accessible, reliable, fair, or competitive. Candidate Obama promised that all federal contracts of more than $25,000 would be competitively bid, but President Obama awarded a no-bid federal contract for more than $24 million.

Only after the president came under intense media scrutiny for awarding the almost $25-million no-bid contract was it rescinded. Obama's State Department spokesperson had this to say about the no-bid contract: "If you want to say this violates the basis on which this administration came into office and campaigned, fair enough."

Once again Candidate Obama promised voters what they wanted to hear—an end to no-bid government contracts—while President Obama awarded hundreds of millions of dollars in that exact type of contract. That's called lying.

At this rate, the only bid voters will want is to bid adieu to another Obama term in the White House.

Read More:

- *http://change.gov/agenda/fiscal_agenda/*
- *http://www.barackobama.com/pdf/issues/fiscal/ObamaPolicy_Fiscal.pdf*
- *http://www.foxnews.com/politics/2010/01/25/obama-administration-steers-lucrative-bid-contract-afghan-work-dem-donor#ixzz1HC33y12G*
- *http://www.foxnews.com/politics/2010/01/25/obama-administration-steers-lucrative-bid-contract-afghan-work-dem-donor#ixzz1HC2rhdtS*
- *http://www.foxnews.com/politics/2010/01/30/cancels-bid-contract-afghan-work-democractic-donor/#ixzz1oAiDepzb*

"I DON'T TAKE MONEY FROM LOBBYISTS"—JUST FROM THEIR SPOUSES

INTELLECTUAL FRAUD: TAKING DONATIONS FROM SPOUSES, CHILDREN, AND EMPLOYEES OF LOBBYISTS

"I DON'T TAKE MONEY FROM LOBBYISTS"

"I don't take money from ... lobbyists, and I won't let them block change anymore."

—Candidate Barack Obama

In the chest of a typical American beats the heart of an idealist who wants elected leaders to answer to a higher standard. While few make the grade, every electoral season offers candidates who openly claim that standard, striking a chord in those hearts and typically winning their votes.

In 2008 Candidate Obama positioned himself as that idealist by putting forth the premise that he didn't "take money from oil companies or Washington lobbyists, and I won't let them block change anymore."

Despite stump speeches and campaign commercials in which he repeated that promise, a review of campaign ethics reports reveals that Candidate Obama was once again parsing the truth to his own advantage. While he may have refused contributions from registered lobbyists, he happily accepted them from their spouses, children, employees, and other associates.

This verbal sleight of hand was yet another example of Candidate Obama's casual relationship with the truth and his willingness to confuse the American people in pursuit of the presidency.

His comfort with this lack of honesty flows from the top down. Asked about the disparity between Obama's pledge to take no money from lobbyists and his acceptance of money from their spouses, Obama's campaign team merely spouted more cloudy rhetoric: "It isn't a perfect solution to the problem, and it isn't even a perfect symbol."

If anything, this episode is the "perfect symbol" of a deceitful candidate promising change to get our vote, then changing nothing.

Obama and his I-don't-take-money-from-lobbyists commercials both fooled the voters and played us for fools.

Read More:

- http://www.factcheck.org/elections-2008/democratic_candidates_debate.html

NEVER LET THE FACTS
STAND IN THE WAY OF TRUTH

LAW PROFESSOR UNABLE TO
READ A JUDGE'S RULING

JUDGES FOUND
OBAMACARE
UNCONSTITUTIONAL

"Keep in mind that we've had twelve judges ... that just threw this case out — the notion that the health care law was unconstitutional."

—President Barack Obama

As the president's health insurance bill, Obamacare, took shape behind closed doors and was passed by Democratic majorities in both the Senate and the House, concerned citizens and their leaders' protests were drowned out by media praise and the majority party's claims of inevitability.

Once the bill was available for review (during such a short time that no hope of change was possible), readers discovered some troubling, even unconstitutional, elements. In subsequent separate court proceedings, two of four presiding judges found the law unconstitutional.

President Obama was a constitutional law professor before running for office, and he is papering over the reality that judges are finding his signature legislation illegal. President Obama seems determined to fool the American people into believing that twelve judges upheld the constitutionality of his signature law establishing Obamacare.

In an on-air interview with Bill O'Reilly of Fox News, President Obama said, "Keep in mind that we've had twelve judges…that just threw this case out—the notion that the health care law was unconstitutional."

Those twelve judges did not hear the merits of Obamacare, nor did they issue a ruling about whether Obamacare is constitutional. Rather, all twelve cases were dismissed for purely procedural reasons.

By omitting mention of the four judges who actually did rule on the merits of the law (and their 50–50 split of opinion), and emphasizing the twelve who dumped the cases before hearing them, President Obama claims a perspective that is disingenuous for a law professor and false for a president.

As a candidate, and now as president, Barack Obama has proven his ability to dismiss honest interpretations of facts and regurgitate what he wants the truth to be rather than the truth itself.

Obamacare may be found constitutional in the end, but of the four judges who've ruled on the merits of its constitutionality, two have found it unconstitutional. To omit this truth is intellectual dishonesty.

Americans deserve an honest debate, not intellectual fraud.

Read More:

• *http://www.politifact.com/truth-o-meter/statements/2011/feb/08/ barack-obama/president-obama-says-12-judges-have-rejected-notio/*

MUSICAL CHAIRS ON HEALTH CARE DEBATE

PUT ALL THE PARTIES IN A ROOM AND BROADCAST NEGOTIATIONS ON C-SPAN

HEALTHCARE TRANSPARENCY

C SPAN

"That's what I will do in bringing all parties together, not negotiating behind closed doors, but bringing all parties together, and broadcasting those negotiations on C-SPAN so that the American people can see what their choices are."

—Candidate Barack Obama

Candidate Obama's campaign frequently touched on voters' concerns about the rising cost of health care and their perception that the outgoing Bush administration operated with undue secrecy. Countless times Candidate Obama promised to have "open and public discussions with all stakeholders" and to "pass health care reform," if we would only elect him president.

As a candidate Obama drew significant applause for his variations on the transparency theme; in one version he stated,

> That's what I will do in bringing all parties together, not negotiating behind closed doors, but bringing all parties together, and broadcasting those negotiations on C-SPAN so that the American people can see what the choices are, because … we have to … enlist the American people in the process.

As is his proven pattern, President Obama broke Candidate Obama's promise.

In crafting his health insurance legislation, Obamacare, President Obama did not enlist C-SPAN or any other news outlet to broadcast discussions with all parties. In fact, President Obama held most of his substantive meetings on health insurance reform behind closed doors, in secret.

Elected officials, and even news outlets that had heaped adoration on Candidate Obama, called President Obama to task for refusing to even discuss the legislation with numerous parties involved, including those voting on the bill.

Despite their protests, President Obama began lobbying for his Obamacare health insurance mandate with two secret, closed-door meetings in which he forced concessions from hospitals and drug companies. When asked about those two secret meetings, Senate Finance Committee Chairman Max Baucus, a key Democrat involved, said, "They were private, yes."

Even the Democratic National Committee, through Obama's group Organizing for America, admitted that the negotiations were secret in an e-mail asking supporters to call their lawmakers and urge them to back Obama's concept of health care reform, Obamacare.

"The behind-the-scenes committee negotiations aren't front-page news," the e-mail said, but it warned that "as we speak, key committees in Congress are weighing options and making final decisions about how to tackle health care reform. This could be one of the last opportunities to shape the legislation before it's written."

There was one token health insurance forum covered on C-SPAN, but it was far from a negotiation with all parties of the sort promised by Candidate Obama. It bore a closer resemblance to a campaign event than an open policy debate.

When asked about the president's pledge for an open and transparent discussion by the interested parties in the health care debate, Obama's press secretary said, "I don't think the president intimated that every decision putting together a health care bill would be on public TV."

Candidate Obama didn't "intimate" a public discussion on health care; he promised voters he'd "broadcast those negotiations on C-SPAN," rather than negotiate "behind closed doors." But he didn't.

Once elected president, he broke the promise he had made as a candidate, ramrodding through what some believe is the most secretive piece of major legislation forced into law in decades. Even the Pulitzer Prize–winning PolitiFact, summarized the President's effort as a flip-flop:

> Obama promised—repeatedly—an end to closed-door negotiations and complete openness for the health care talks. But he hasn't delivered. Instead of open talks on C-SPAN, we've gotten more of the same—talks behind closed doors at the White House and Congress.

Here we have yet another passionate promise from Candidate Obama broken by the same man once we elected him president.

Candidate Obama's commitment to transparency in the health care debate appears to have been a means to drive up vote tallies. The only thing transparent about President Obama's efforts is the clear fact that he lied. When it comes to Obama's claims of transparency we must ask if *lies* are the window to the soul.

Read More:

• http://www.politifact.com/truth-o-meter/promises/obameter/promise/517/health-care-reform-public-sessions-C-SPAN/

LOSE YOUR HOUSE?
YOUR VOTES GAVE ME MINE

HE TOOK THE WHITE HOUSE,
THEN IGNORED HIS PROMISE AS
WE LOST OURS

"Barack Obama will repeal this provision so ordinary families can also get relief that bankruptcy laws were intended to provide."

—Candidate Barack Obama's Campaign literature

As economic clouds gathered throughout the 2008 presidential campaign, home foreclosures mounted. Candidate Obama portrayed himself as the champion of the poor and working classes. He gained votes and campaign contributions by convincing voters—particularly poor and working-class ones—that he would change bankruptcy laws so that their homes would be protected during financial distress.

Obama explained:

> While investors who own multiple homes and people with vacation homes can renegotiate those mortgages in bankruptcy, current Chapter 13 law prohibits bankruptcy judges from modifying the original terms of home mortgages for ordinary families—regardless of whether the loan was predatory or unfair or is otherwise unaffordable.

Obama's campaign material reiterated this pledge: "Barack Obama will repeal this provision so ordinary families can also get relief that bankruptcy laws were intended to provide."

According to Candidate Obama, repealing that provision "could prevent as many as 600,000 homeowners from being foreclosed upon."

During his first two and a half years in office, President Obama watched home foreclosures and bankruptcies skyrocket, but he failed to keep his promise to "repeal this provision" of the bankruptcy code.

As a result of Candidate Obama's empty words and President Obama's failure to act, countless American families have lost their homes. Ordinary families across America took Obama at his word while he took our votes, and now we're unfairly harmed, as unemployment hits generational highs and home foreclosures and gas prices are higher than ordinary families ever imagined.

In an unfortunate twist, President Obama's broken promise may aid in his reelection. Voter registration cards mailed to the foreclosed homes of his former supporters may not catch up with these displaced families in time for them to vote against him in 2012.

Read More:

• http://www.barackobama.com/pdf/issues/UrbanFactSheet.pdf
• http://www.politifact.com/truth-o-meter/promises/obameter/promise/313/allow-bankruptcy-judges-to-modify-terms-of-a-home-/

HOUSTON, WE HAVE A PROBLEM!

SENDING PRO-NASA VOTERS INTO ORBIT

"Here's what I'm committing to: continue Constellation. We're going to close the gap [between the end of the shuttle flight and the next program, Constellation]."

—Candidate Barack Obama

During his campaign, Candidate Obama spoke to large crowds of voters dependent on NASA's continued space programs and made this pledge:

> Under my watch, NASA will inspire the world once again and is going to help grow the economy right here in Brevard County. Here's what I'm committing to: Continue Constellation.

That's why President Obama's cancellation of the Constellation program came as such a shock to the families of Florida who gave Obama their vote.

In keeping with Candidate Obama's shrewd political calculus, he campaigned in the closely divided state of Florida, perhaps the most sought after electorate in 2008, and targeted voters whose jobs and personal welfare were directly related to NASA's space programs. He continued:

> We're going to close the gap [between the end of the shuttle flight and the next program, Constellation].

> We cannot cede our leadership in space. That's why I will help close the gap and ensure that our space program doesn't suffer when the shuttle goes out of service … and by making sure that all those who work in the space industry in Florida do not lose their jobs when the shuttle is retired because we cannot afford to lose their expertise.

In keeping with President Obama's track record of breaking

Candidate Obama's promises, the president's cancellation of NASA's space program was such an about-face that Neil Armstrong, the first man to walk on the Moon, wrote an open letter to the president.

> America is faced with the near-simultaneous ending of the Shuttle program and your recent budget proposal to cancel the Constellation program. This is wrong for our country for many reasons. We are very concerned about America ceding its hard-earned global leadership in space technology to other nations. We are stunned that, in a time of economic crisis, this move will force as many as 30,000 irreplaceable engineers and managers out of the space industry.

PolitiFact, the Pulitzer Prize-winning journalistic entity that rates candidates' claims and actions, had this to say about Obama's flip-flop on the Constellation program:

> This change of plans clearly breaks Obama's promise to "endorse the goal of sending human missions to the moon by 2020, as a precursor in an orderly progression to missions to more distant destinations, including Mars."

President Obama's track record isn't just one of broken promises. It's obvious that he says anything to get elected, only to make decisions regardless of his words once elected.

Americans deserve better.

Read More:

- http://blogs.orlandosentinel.com/news_space_thewritestuff/2010/04/griffin-nasa-luminaries-urge-obama-to-change-space-policy.html
- http://www.scientificamerican.com/article.cfm?id=nasa-budget-constellation-cancel
- http://my.barackobama.com/page/community/post/amandascott/gG5kBP
- http://www.msnbc.msn.com/id/36476183/ns/technology_and_science-space/t/first-moonwalker-blasts-obamas-space-plan/

WHO NEEDS THE AUTISTIC VOTE ANYWAY?

FAILED TO "FULLY FUND" COMBATING AUTISM ACT

COMBATING AUTISM ACT
missing the mark

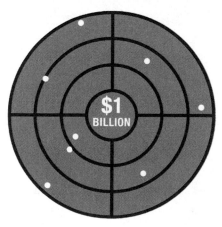

$1 BILLION

"[I promise to] fully fund the Combating Autism Act, which provides nearly $1 billion in autism-related funding over five years, [and] appoint a federal autism spectrum disorders (ASD) coordinator to oversee federal ASD ... efforts."

—Candidate Barack Obama

Like many charismatic leaders, Candidate Obama oozed empathy for voters struggling with challenges of every kind. In one of his more touching moments he reached out to families with autistic children, promising to "fully fund the Combating Autism Act, which provides nearly $1 billion in autism-related funding over five years" and to "appoint a federal autism spectrum disorders (ASD) coordinator."

Once elected president he did neither.

President Bush signed the Combating Autism Act (CAA) into law on December 26, 2006. It allowed for $920 million in new federal funding over five years for this worthy cause. However, the president and Congress must actually allocate those dollars, which is why Obama campaigned on "fully funding" the CAA.

That five-year window to fully fund the CAA closed at the end of the federal government's 2011 fiscal year, on June 30. President Obama failed to make good on his promise of fully funding autism research.

Even worse, once elected, our president failed to appoint an ASD coordinator. This failing is worse because appointing a coordinator doesn't require any funds from Congress—this appointment is within his power as president.

What's striking is that Candidate Obama had a solution for almost every affliction, typically in the form of a new commission, a new budget allotment, or a new approach to doing business. In most cases these solutions were never even mentioned after he won the election.

In seeking votes, Candidate Obama promised the parents of autistic children that he would "appoint a federal autism spectrum disorders (ASD) coordinator to oversee federal ASD ... efforts." Now in the final year of his term, in what has become a tragic pattern, Obama has yet to keep this promise. For a president more prone to appointing "czars" than any before him, this should have been a simple promise to keep.

If there were an autism coordinator, perhaps Obama would have been able to keep his other promise: to fully fund the Combat Autism Act.

There is no excuse for President Obama to dole out trillions of dollars to Wall Street banks, AIG, General Motors, and other "stimulus" recipients while failing to keep his promise to fully fund the Combating Autism Act.

However, it's an affront to not, at the very least, appoint an autism coordinator. As Obama seeks reelection, how are we to trust what he says during this campaign, when he so thoroughly failed to keep his word after the last campaign?

Whether Candidate Obama had no grasp of the challenges of the presidency or deliberately misled Americans to get their votes, his path is littered with heartbroken American families and broken promises.

Read More:

- *http://www.barackobama.com/pdf/AutismSpectrumDisorders.pdf*
- *http://www.autismspeaks.org/government_affairs/combating_autism_ act.php*
- *http://www.disabled-world.com/disability/statistics/caa-funding-allocations.php*

REASON (31)

CONGRESS AND AMERICA KNOW WHAT I TELL THEM

PUSHING INACCURATE DATA ON CONGRESS AND AMERICA

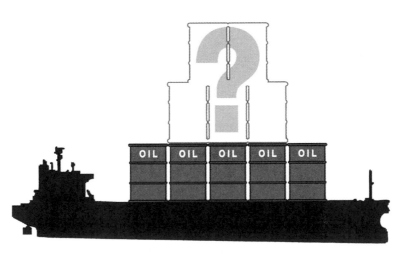

OBAMA SAYS WE IMPORT MORE OIL THAN EVER

"We import more oil today than ever before."(FALSE)

—President Barack Obama

As a candidate, Obama regularly attacked oil companies and decried our nation's need for foreign oil. During his campaign and since his election, Obama has consistently made false statements about oil—both regarding his close ties to large oil companies and in inaccurate and conflicting proclamations about oil consumption.

Regarding oil, Obama cites inaccurate statistics with great conviction and displays some of his most disturbing examples of hypocrisy (see "I Am Not a Crook..." and "Somebody Tell OPEC the End is Nigh").

The examples of Obama's fibs and flip-flops on oil are almost too long to list, but some highlights follow.

Obama claimed during a rally in Wisconsin that his energy plan would "stop us from sending $700 billion a year to tyrants and dictators for their oil."

According to the Associated Press, "The claim, however, wildly exaggerates the amount of money going to unfriendly nations" and was at least $200 billion more than the actual amount. That means Candidate Obama's claim exaggerated reality by at least 25 percent.

Perhaps most disturbing was President Obama's first joint address to Congress. He used false data to chastise Congress for the country's excessive use of oil. Obama claimed, "We import more oil today than ever before" (February 24, 2009). Obama's statement, however, was false.

In reality, U.S. oil imports peaked in 2005 and are down approximately 25 percent from November of that year. It's disturbing that Obama uses inaccurate data to pressure Congress to reduce our dependence on foreign oil. This alone should give us pause as to Obama's credibility on oil, but his actions invoke even greater concern.

After endlessly proclaiming his commitment to reduce America's dependence on foreign oil and wildly exaggerating before Congress and America, Obama then flew to Brazil to discuss its increase in oil production. He publicly declared to Brazilian oil companies, "We want to be your best customer."

Though he cites false data to Congress, in reality President Obama will say whatever it takes for a sound bite, to win a vote, or retain power.

Read More:

- *http://www.whitehouse.gov/the_press_office/Transcript-of-President-Obamas-Interview-with-Novaya-Gazeta/*
- *http://factcheck.org/2009/07/same-inaccurate-claim-on-oil-imports/*
- *http://www.chron.com/disp/story.mpl/business/energy/6063031.html*

CAMPAIGN AS ROBIN HOOD; RULE AS PINOCCHIO

FAILED TO RAISE THE MINIMUM WAGE TO $9.50

"As President, [I] will further raise the minimum wage to $9.50 an hour by 2011."

—Candidate Barack Obama

Observers of Candidate Obama's presidential campaign could be excused for experiencing déjà vu as he utilized the populist sentiments of Robin Hood.

Not only did Candidate Obama promise that "only the rich would see their taxes increase," he vowed to give to the poor by raising the national minimum wage to $9.50 an hour by 2011.

President Obama broke both those promises.

Obama extended the "Bush tax cuts for the rich" through the end of his term and failed to advance a minimum wage increase. As a candidate Obama professed to be Robin Hood, but as president he has acted more like Pinocchio.

The minimum wage issue was a favorite standby of Candidate Obama at campaign stops across America, but President Obama has failed to stand by his promise to low-income American workers.

With 2011 having come and gone, it's clear that President Obama broke faith with America's workers and failed to keep Candidate Obama's promise to raise the minimum wage to $9.50 an hour by 2011.

Candidate Obama told voters that $9.50 an hour was needed to earn "a living wage that allows them to raise their families and pay for basic needs such as food, transportation, and housing." President Obama then extended the "Bush tax cuts for the rich" and failed to act on increasing the minimum wage.

Sadly, voters who bought into the idea of Obama as Robin Hood have been robbed of their optimism since Obama was elected president.

Read More:

- *http://www.barackobama.com/pdf/issues/UrbanFactSheet.pdf*
- *http://change.gov/agenda/poverty_agenda/*

"DISCHARGE MEDICAL EXPENSES IN BANKRUPTCY"... PYSCHE!

NO DISCHARGE FOR MEDICAL EXPENSES IN BANKRUPTCY, EVEN THOUGH CANDIDATE OBAMA PROMISED OTHERWISE

OBAMA PROMISED TO
PROTECT AGAINST
MEDICAL BANKRUPTCY

"[I will] allow the discharge of medical expenses in bankruptcy."

—Candidate Barack Obama

Candidate Obama promised to create an exemption that would allow bankruptcy judges to eliminate debts created by medical expenses. Under existing bankruptcy regulations, medical debts are usually paid over time. Candidate Obama made a promise to allow medical expenses to be discharged in bankruptcy rather than have people put on extended payment plans.

President Obama: promise broken.

In his endless quest for votes and campaign contributions, Candidate Obama took aim at medical insurance companies, targeting skyrocketing medical expenses as a significant problem in America (his polling, no doubt, supported that premise).

Obama's emotional pleas, citing stories of families ruined by crushing medical bills, moved compassionate Americans. He implied that he, and only he, could provide relief to those being driven to bankruptcy by medical expenses if only we elected him president.

Many families struggling against bankruptcy are also burdened with the high cost of prescription medicine and were seeking cheaper drugs in Canada and elsewhere. Obama also offered hope on this front by promising the legal import of those, if only we'd elect him—yet another campaign promise Obama broke upon becoming president (see "Sick People Should Pay More").

Unfortunately for those on the brink of bankruptcy due to medical expenses, the president we elected forgot his promise, ensuring Americans got stuck with the check.

Read More:

• *http://www.barackobama.com/pdf/issues/UrbanFactSheet.pdf*

NO MORE PARTISANSHIP EXCEPT WHEN I DEEM IT NECESSARY

PRESIDENT OBAMA FINDS A SCAPEGOAT IN THE OPPOSING PARTY

"Find Republican members of Congress on Twitter, call them out and demand they pass this bill."

—President Barack Obama's reelection campaign

In the hands of a skilled politico, false piety is wonderful for energizing one's base, but it is also especially damaging to good governance. Despite professing a devotion to a higher level of statesmanship and noble governance on the campaign trail, President Obama has proven a master at the polarizing tactics of partisanship, wielding it to slur opponents and raise money while disregarding its harmful impact on our nation's future.

His artful and shameless mastery of partisanship can best be seen in the debate surrounding his recent jobs bill.

When the Republican minority in the Senate repeatedly called for a vote on the president's jobs bill, the Democratic majority refused (reportedly due to fears of insufficient support among Senate Democrats).

Later that very day Obama's unabashed partisanship manifested itself as an attack on Republicans in Congress, which took the form of a fundraising e-mail from his campaign.

It read, in part:

> It's not clear which part of the bill [Republicans] now object to: building roads, hiring teachers, getting veterans back to work. They're willing to block the American Jobs Act—and they think you won't do anything about it.
>
> **But here's something you can do: Find Republican members of Congress on Twitter, call them out, and demand they pass this bill.**

Conspicuously absent from the president's attack on Republicans is any mention of the failure to allow a vote on his jobs bill in the Senate, and he ignored entirely Republican senators' calls for a vote.

The hypocrisy was so blatant that even the Associated Press pointed out the obvious by saying:

> In President Barack Obama's sales pitch for his jobs bill, there are two versions of reality: The one in his speeches and the one actually unfolding in Washington.

> When Obama accuses Republicans of standing in the way of his nearly $450 billion plan, he ignores the fact that his own party has struggled to unite behind the proposal.

Repeatedly attacking Republicans for Democratic acts is the very definition of partisan politics and a genuine impediment to the progress he promised the American people.

This pattern of unabashed partisanship and hypocrisy moves through issues like warrantless wiretaps, earmarks, and closing Guantánamo, leaving in its wake a nation less trusting of its government and deeply troubled about the future.

America most definitely deserves better than partisanship; we deserve honest leaders advancing honest solutions.

Read More:

- *http://news.yahoo.com/spin-meter-obama-disconnects-rhetoric-reality-081418391.html*
- *http://www.weeklystandard.com/blogs/obama-campaign-says-gop-blocking-jobs-bill-after-reid-blocks-jobs-bill_595022.html*

THE INCONVENIENT TRUTH: ETHICS FAILURE IN OBAMA-LAND

FAILED TO CREATE HIS PROMISED ONLINE LOBBYIST, ETHICS, AND CAMPAIGN FINANCE DATABASE

CENTRALIZED INTERNET DATABASE
ETHICS REFORM

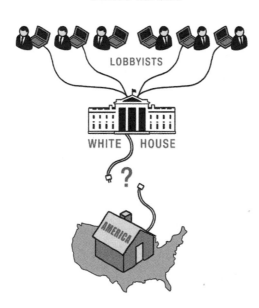

"[I promise] to create a centralized Internet database of lobbying reports, ethics records, and campaign finance filings."

—Candidate Barack Obama

Candidate Obama campaigned on a commitment to "increase ethics in Washington." Obama implied that the outgoing president had ethics problems, as did those who had been in Washington for a while, like his Republican opponent, John McCain. They were all part of a corrupt Washington establishment.

Obama portrayed himself as the squeaky clean outsider. During the campaign Obama aggressively attacked Senator McCain for having "no less than 177 lobbyists working on his campaign."

To draw a distinction between himself and McCain, Obama promised to "create a centralized Internet database of lobbying reports, ethics records, and campaign finance filings" and to "fight for an independent agency to oversee the investigation of congressional ethics violations."

Once elected, President Obama failed to keep his promise to create an Internet database. In an equally disturbing about-face, Obama appointed a cadre of lobbyists to his cabinet and senior administration positions (see "Lobby for a Job?").

Once again, Candidate Obama was skilled at talking the talk, but President Obama is incapable or unwilling to walk the walk.

Read More:

- *http://www.barackobama.com/issues/index_campaign.php*
- *http://www.politifact.com/truth-o-meter/promises/obameter/ promise/230/centralize-ethics-and-lobbying-information-for-vot/*

HOPELESS DREAMS FOR AFTERSCHOOL PROGRAMS

"SOCCER MOMS"—I'LL BUY YOUR VOTE; YOU BUY YOUR OWN PROGRAM

HOPELESS DREAMS FOR
AFTERSCHOOL PROGRAMS

"[I promise to] double funding for the main federal support for afterschool programs ... to serve one million more children."

—Candidate Barack Obama

Candidate Obama crisscrossed the country in 2008, seeking votes and speaking to adoring crowds. He courted the critical soccer mom vote with a bold promise to "double funding for the main federal support for afterschool programs, the 21st Century Community Learning Centers program, to serve one million more children."

Unfortunately for those children, President Obama failed to honor that promise. He didn't even ask Congress to appropriate more for the program in 2010 than he had in 2009. Now in his third budget as president, Obama has failed to pursue these increases from Congress.

In fact, the U.S. House recently added $50 million to the program, over and above what the president sought. While both President Obama and Congress have spent wildly in other areas, only the U.S. House had the will to propose increasing funding for the 21st Century Community Learning Centers program.

The abandonment of this promise demonstrates that Obama is taking both voters and schoolchildren for granted. We took Obama at his word and he took us for a ride. What will he do with another four years?

Read More:

- *http://change.gov/agenda/education_agenda/*
- *http://www2.ed.gov/about/overview/budget/budget10/10action.pdf*
- *http://www.politifact.com/truth-o-meter/promises/obameter/promise/249/double-funding-for-afterschool-programs/*

BORDER INSECURITY?

CAMPAIGNED ON TOUGH BORDER STANCE, THEN STOOD DOWN ON BORDER SECURITY

"[I promise] lasting and dedicated security to our borders [and to] do a better job patrolling the Canadian and Mexican borders."

—Candidate Barack Obama

As reports of shootouts and mass executions in Mexico's ongoing drug cartel wars raised tension levels across the United States, Candidate Obama tapped into that apprehension with tough talk about border security, promising to provide a "lasting and dedicated security to our borders."

Since elected, President Obama has not merely underachieved but seemingly sought to reduce border security by fighting funding for the border fence and reducing our National Guard's presence on the southern border by 75 percent, from twelve hundred to three hundred.

Some three years after President Obama took office, the nonpartisan Government Accountability Office (GAO) estimated that the Border Patrol has only 44 percent of our nation's southwest border secured. In short, the federal agency tasked with securing our southernmost boundary, which stretches from San Diego, California, to Brownsville, Texas, lacks operational control of more than eleven hundred miles.

Adding insult to his injurious border security policy, President Obama had the audacity to scold and mock border security advocates in a May 2011 speech in El Paso, Texas:

> We have gone above and beyond what was requested by the very Republicans who said they supported broader reform as long as we got serious about enforcement.

But even though we've answered these concerns, I gotta say I suspect there are still going to be some who are trying to move the goalposts on us one more time. Maybe they'll need a moat. Maybe they'll want alligators in the moat.

Americans, whose safety is threatened by an unsecured border, deserve better than mockery. They deserve a chief executive who keeps his promises and esteems border security over political expediency.

Sadly, yet true to form, as a candidate Obama made lofty promises to secure the border when what he wanted to secure was more votes.

Read More:

- *http://www.gao.gov/htext/d11374t.html*
- *http://www.usatoday.com/news/military/story/2011-12-20/national-guard-border-mexico/52124718/1*
- *http://www.foxnews.com/politics/2011/05/10/obama-urges-congress-pass-immigration-reform/*

SICK BUT CAN'T AFFORD TO MISS WORK? VOTE FOR ME

DESPITE PROMISE, NO SEVEN DAYS OF PAID SICK LEAVE

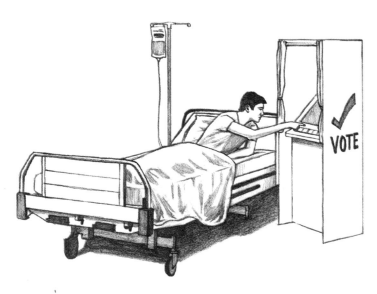

SICK DAYS PROMISE...BROKEN

"Barack Obama and Joe Biden will require that all employers provide seven paid sick days a year."

—Candidate Barack Obama's campaign materials

O bama campaigned as the candidate of the average working-class American, even though he's a Harvard Law School graduate and millionaire who sends his children to private schools.

As his campaign picked up steam and the American economy slowed, Obama drew upon his experience as an inner-city community organizer, touting a number of initiatives that attacked business and at the same time appealed to working-class Americans.

Obama went on the offensive over unpaid sick leave, as if he himself were a factory worker. Enough of those workers believed his rhetoric to help in electing him president.

Candidate Obama spoke like a union representative, promising seven paid sick days of leave a year. But he's ruled like a scab since the election, with no action on his pledge and all but ignoring the working class who elected him.

Candidate Obama drew loud cheers for his plan to "require that all employers provide seven paid sick days a year" while also promising home mortgage relief and bankruptcy protections for the poor (see "No Mortgage on White House, Not My Problem" and "Lose Your House? Your Votes Gave Me Mine"). Each promise is still unfulfilled, of course.

Candidate Obama's printed campaign materials stated: "Half of all private sector workers have no paid sick days and the problem is worse for employees in low-paying jobs where less than a quarter receive any paid sick days. Barack Obama and Joe Biden will require that employers provide seven paid sick days per year."

It's been more than three years since Candidate Obama became President Obama. His election was made possible in part by Americans without paid sick leave, who were optimistic about getting it.

Hopefully, those of us who lack paid sick leave have not needed it since Obama became president because his promise to "require that all employers provide seven paid sick days a year" is still only an unfulfilled promise.

Read More:

• *http://www.barackobama.com/pdf/issues/UrbanFactSheet.pdf*

REASON 39

BUT IRAQI REFUGEES DON'T VOTE ...

PROMISE MADE FOR POLITICAL GAIN; PROMISE IGNORED ONCE ELECTED

"[I promise to] form an international working group to help [displaced Iraqis]."

—Candidate Barack Obama

During the 2008 campaign, Obama addressed the global war on terror in terms tailored for a specific audience: the liberal left and so-called soccer moms whose empathy for Iraqi refugees was palpable. Candidate Obama gave lip service to gain their votes, only to ignore his promise once elected.

The 2008 presidential campaign took place in the broader context of the wars in Iraq and Afghanistan with the full-color consequences broadcast nightly into American living rooms.

As the compassion candidate Obama worked diligently to distinguish himself on the Iraq issue, glossing over the causes, maligning the military involvement, and waxing eloquently on stories of countless Iraqis whose lives were disrupted by our "unconstitutional" invasion. Obama's strategy to meet his political needs and his solution to the problem of Iraqi refugees, were his repeated promises to "form an international working group" to help them.

On Election Day legions of soccer moms did vote to turn Candidate Obama into President Obama. Unfortunately for them and, more important, those five million or so refugees who fled to Syria, Jordan, and other nations, President Obama seems to have forgotten this heartfelt promise and others.

As of this writing, there is no working group for Iraqi refugees, and if President Obama's track record is any indication, there won't be one any time soon.

Read More:

• *http://www.politifact.com/truth-o-meter/promises/obameter/ promise/129/form-international-group-to-help-iraq-refugees/*

I WAS FOR THE DEBT CEILING; BEFORE I WAS AGAINST THE DEBT CEILING

FLIP-FLOPPED ON RAISING THE DEBT CEILING

"RAISING AMERICA'S DEBT LIMIT = LEADERSHIP FAILURE"
-OBAMA

"America has a debt problem and a failure of leadership. Americans deserve better. I therefore intend to oppose the effort to increase America's debt limit."

—U.S. Senator Barack Obama

While many contrasts between Candidate Obama and President Obama have been cited, there are also repeated instances of President Obama abandoning positions he once vigorously defended as a U.S. senator. One that is especially worrisome for future generations is the 180-degree turn he executed on the federal government's debt ceiling.

Less than three years before he became president, Senator Obama went on record scolding his congressional colleagues for their desire to raise the debt ceiling to allow for more government spending. Sounding like a fiscal conservative, he presented a compelling argument for choosing fiscal discipline over raising the debt ceiling.

> The fact that we are here today to debate raising America's debt limit is a sign of leadership failure ... Leadership means that "the buck stops here." Instead, Washington is shifting the burden of bad choices today onto the backs of our children and grandchildren. America has a debt problem and a failure of leadership. Americans deserve better. I therefore intend to oppose the effort to increase America's debt limit (March 16, 2006).

One would expect that such a principled orator, having articulated such strongly held beliefs about government's responsibility to future generations, would take a leadership role on the issue after becoming president.

Unfortunately, just a few years later, such concerns have apparently evaporated in the face of political expediency.

Instead of continued calls for discipline and tough choices, President Obama is using his typical, aggressive rhetoric on Congress in his attempts to raise the debt ceiling.

It appears that Obama will point fingers when someone else is spending wildly, but when his hand is on the purse strings and his spending is questioned, those questioners are "playing politics."

Whether he's insinuating that members of Congress are acting childishly in refusing to raise the limit or admonishing them not to "play politics," President Obama made it his mission to get the debt limit raised to fund his spending programs.

Senator Obama was right: "The fact that we are here today to debate raising America's debt limit is a sign of leadership failure." There is a leadership failure today. True leaders honor their words and protect our children's future from crushing debt rather than burden them by mortgaging our nation.

If only President Obama would keep Senator Obama's word. Then our children might not be facing such a bleak future. We voted for hope and change only to elect partisan hypocrisy.

Read More:

- *http://www.cbsnews.com/8301-503544_162-20027412-503544.html*
- *http://www.nationalreview.com/corner/256199/obama-not-always-fan-upping-debt-ceiling-katrina-trinko*
- *http://www.barackobama.com/pdf/issues/fiscal/ObamaPolicy_Fiscal.pdf*

REASON 41

A FORMER CONSTITUTIONAL LAWYER IGNORES FEDERAL LAWS

ENTHUSIASTICALLY ENFORCES HIS OBAMACARE LAW WHILE NO LONGER DEFENDING A LAW CONCERNING MARRIAGE

FEDERAL LAW HYPOCRISY

OBAMACARE

DEFENSE OF
MARRIAGE ACT

President Obama instructed the Justice Department to stop defending the constitutionality of the Defense of Marriage Act.

Congress passes bills and the president either signs these bills into law or vetoes them; this prevents them from becoming law. The Defense of Marriage Act (DOMA), a law defining marriage as between one man and one woman, was enacted by overwhelming support in the Congress: DOMA passed 85 to 14 in the Senate and 342 to 67 in the House. Clearly Congress thought it a wise and constitutional law, as over 80 percent of Congress voted for it. Until a law is repealed or found unconstitutional by the U.S. Supreme Court, it is the duty of the executive branch (the president and all his appointees) to defend and enforce each law.

The judicial branch, headed by the U.S. Supreme Court, has the power to determine whether a law passed by Congress and signed by the president is unconstitutional.

Once a bill becomes a law, the executive branch has the duty to defend the constitutionality of that law in court and to enforce that law.

The operative word here is "duty." The executive branch has a duty to defend these laws. If the executive branch, Congress, or the citizenry feels that a law needs to be changed or removed entirely, then a bill must be passed to repeal that law. Until a repeal or the U.S. Supreme Court finds the law unconstitutional the president must defend the law in court.

Obama simply decided that the 1996 law defining marriage as

between a man and a woman was unconstitutional, and ordered his attorney general to stop defending the law in court. This law was passed by Congress and signed by President Clinton in 1996, and has been enforced ever since it was passed.

Obama displays a shocking arrogance by declaring a law unconstitutional and acting on that determination, as it's the role of the Supreme Court to decide whether a federal law is unconstitutional.

Obama is obviously comfortable with the hypocrisy of choosing not to defend the Defense of Marriage Act while fully defending his Obamacare legislation. More than one federal judge has ruled Obamacare to be unconstitutional, yet Obama continues to ignore these rulings and instructs his executive branch appointees to fervently defend Obamacare while abandoning the Defense of Marriage Act.

Both the Defense of Marriage Act and Obamacare have been challenged in federal courts, with federal judges finding both laws unconstitutional. However, the Supreme Court has not ruled in either case. The executive branch should defend a law passed by Congress and signed by the president until the Supreme Court rules it unconstitutional.

Only the Supreme Court has the absolute authority to decide if a law is constitutional. A president cannot arbitrarily decide the constitutionality of an issue.

Determining constitutionality is the role of federal courts. We have three separate branches of government: the legislative branch (Congress) makes laws; the executive branch (the president) enforces laws; and the judicial branch (the federal courts, led by the Supreme Court) rules on the laws' constitutionality.

President Obama's comfort with his own hypocrisy, in enforcing a law he likes (Obamacare) while no longer defending a law he doesn't (the Defense of Marriage Act), has become all too common.

How are Americans supposed to support our president when he arbitrarily refuses to defend some laws and vigorously defends others?

Read More:

- *http://www.nytimes.com/2011/02/24/us/24marriage.html*
- *http://abcnews.go.com/Politics/obama-administration-drops-legal-defense-marriage-act/story?id=12981242*

OUT TO LUNCH
(WITH LOBBYISTS—SHHHHH)

HOLD MEETINGS OUTSIDE THE
WHITE HOUSE SO PUBLIC WON'T KNOW

"[Lobbyists] will not run my White House. You'll help me run my White House [as the] most transparent White House in history."

—Candidate Barack Obama

Senior White House aides hold secret meetings with lobbyists outside the White House so the meetings aren't recorded in the White House visitor log. Where's the transparency?

Candidate Obama campaigned on eliminating the influence of lobbyists in the White House. He promised he would "not take campaign donations from lobbyists," and he would "not allow lobbyists who work in his White House to regulate their recent employers." He also promised to have the "most transparent White House in history."

We know that Obama took donations from lobbyists' spouses and employees (see "'I Don't Take Money from Lobbyists'—Just from Their Spouses"), and has more than forty former lobbyists working in senior administration positions (many were granted waivers from his policy of regulating recent employers). Now we learn that senior White House officials are meeting lobbyists off-site, which keeps those meetings from showing up in the White House visitor log.

Where is the Obama who claimed his administration would be committed to creating "an unprecedented level of openness in government?"

The Washington, DC-based Politico said:

> Caught between their boss's antilobbyist rhetoric and the reality of governing, President Barack Obama's aides often steer meetings with lobbyists to a complex just off the White House grounds—and several of the lobbyists involved say they believe the choice of venue is no accident.

It allows the Obama administration to keep these lobbyist meetings shielded from public view—and out of Secret Service logs kept on visitors to the White House and later released to the public.

Obama bemoaned the influence of lobbyists and promised to reduce their influence, and to run a White House for the people, not for special interests.

Now that he's elected, senior administration officials are running to an off-site location to meet lobbyists so there's no record of the meeting in the White House visitor log.

According to *The New York Times,* there have been "hundreds" of these secret meetings.

Other top Obama fundraisers received millions in stimulus money and key political posts, and have driven Obama's national policy through special-access meetings.

Here's what Politico said about top donors who got White House jobs:

> Telecom executive Donald H. Gips raised a big bundle of cash to help finance his friend Barack Obama's run for the presidency.
>
> Gips, a vice president of Colorado-based Level 3 Communications, delivered more than $500,000 in contributions for the Obama war chest, while two other company executives collected at least $150,000 more.
>
> After the election, Gips was put in charge of hiring in the Obama White House, helping to place loyalists and fundraisers in many key positions. Then, in mid-2009, Obama named him ambassador to South Africa.
>
> More than two years after Obama took office vowing to banish "special interests" from his administration, nearly 200 of his biggest donors have landed plum government jobs and advisory posts.

What happened to the Obama who said:

> You need leadership you can trust to work for you, not for
> the special interests who have had their thumb on the scale.
> And together we will tell Washington, and their lobbyists,
> that their days of setting the agenda are over. They have
> not funded my campaign. You have. They will not run my
> White House. You'll help me run my White House.

Where is Candidate Obama? I liked him.

We trusted his words only to learn we can't trust him
as president.

Read More:

• http://www.whitehouse.gov/the_press_office/
  TransparencyandOpenGovernment/
• http://www.whitehouse.gov/the-press-office/ExecutiveOrder-
  EthicsCommitments/
• http://www.nytimes.com/2010/06/25/us/politics/25caribou.html
• http://www.politico.com/news/stories/0211/50081.html
• http://www.politico.com/news/stories/0611/56993.html

PAYDAYS FOR PAUPERS

UP TO 50 PERCENT OF ANNUAL SALARY IN BONUSES FOR GM'S EXECUTIVES WHILE OWING THE TAXPAYERS BILLIONS.

GOVERNMENT MOTORS

BONUSES TO EXECUTIVES
=
50% OF SALARIES

"[I will] protect the jobs and benefits of workers and retirees when corporations file for bankruptcy by telling companies that they cannot issue bonuses for executives during bankruptcy while their workers watch their pensions disappear."

—Candidate Barack Obama

General Motors still owes its largest shareholder, the federal government, billions of dollars. This money was partially funded by U.S. taxpayers, with the rest through deficit spending by a government as broke as the beleaguered carmaker.

As a candidate, Obama promised he would "protect the jobs and benefits of workers and retirees when corporations file for bankruptcy."

Candidate Obama talked a lot about protecting the interests of the working man and about defending us against corporate executives who issue themselves astronomical bonuses while our pensions dwindle and the companies reorganize themselves in bankruptcy. But once elected, Obama didn't back up all that talk with actions.

President Obama loaned over $30 billion in taxpayer money to General Motors as GM went through a "controlled bankruptcy," only to stand mute as GM gave bonuses of up to 50 percent to its executives when they still owed the taxpayers over $25 billion.

As a candidate, Obama attacked executive compensation and bailouts with righteous indignation. As president, he showed the voters his indignation by rewarding these same failed executives with millions of dollars in salaries, bonuses, and severances.

- Rick Wagoner, GM's former chairman and chief executive, who led the company during its failure and into bankruptcy, was rewarded by the Obama administration with an $8.2 million severance and a lifetime of benefits payments.

- Fritz Henderson, the chief financial officer of GM when it went broke, was promoted to president and chief operating officer by the Obama administration. Later Henderson resigned and was paid almost $3,000 *an hour* for part-time work in 2010.

Again, as a candidate Obama told Americans what we wanted to hear. As president, Obama did the usual—he broke his word and paid tens of millions of dollars to corporate executives of failed businesses.

Someday maybe I'll drive a car company into the ground and be lucky enough to win the government lottery too.

Read More:

- *http://www.nytimes.com/2011/02/12/business/economy/12auto.html*
- *http://www.politifact.com/truth-o-meter/promises/obameter/ promise/45/forbid-companies-in-bankruptcy-from-giving-executi/*
- *http://abcnews.go.com/Blotter/story?id=7208201&page=1*

REASON 44

OBAMA'S READ-MY-LIPS MOMENT

"REPEAL THE BUSH TAX CUTS FOR THE RICH"... OR NOT

READ MY LIPS, NOT MY MIND...

"I will roll back the Bush tax cuts on people making over $250,000 a year ... Yes, I'm going to roll back the Bush tax cuts for the very wealthiest Americans ... those making $250,000 a year."

—*Candidate Barack Obama*

By the time Barack Obama hit the presidential campaign trail he was blessed with an easy target: an outgoing president who was alienated from the public.

Playing off widespread negative opinions about the president, Obama had merely to attack George W. Bush to elicit applause and support.

One favorite Obama tactic was to attack what he described as "Bush's tax cuts for the rich." He targeted the tax cuts that a narrow segment of Americans making $250,000 or more were receiving and repeatedly pledged to "roll back the Bush tax cuts for the rich."

As part of a likely effort to divert attention from his background as a Harvard Law graduate, Obama repeatedly sounded this populist note, along with his pledge to close the detention facility for alleged terrorists at Guantánamo Bay (see "Did I Say That?").

Even if you've read only a few pages preceding this one, it should come as no surprise that our forty-fourth president failed miserably on both counts.

With the Bush tax cuts set to expire on December 31, 2010, it would have required both chambers of Congress to pass a bill to extend them and Obama choosing to not veto that bill for those cuts to continue into 2011 or beyond.

Despite his derisive assault on the Bush tax cuts as a candidate, once elected, Obama coerced Democrats in the House and Senate into passing a bill to extend those once-mocked tax cuts.

Had he any regard for his repeated promises (or integrity, for that matter), Obama could have kept his word, and those tax cuts would have expired on their own. Instead, he and his team ramrodded the tax cuts through the Democrat-controlled Senate, and then Obama signed that extension into law.

Keeping his campaign promise would have merely required him to cross his arms and wait patiently for the tax cuts to expire. Instead, he took a proactive role in shattering that pledge.

This is yet another example of a candidate promising the moon to win votes and then deliberately breaking his word once in power. It gives one pause to wonder if our forty-fourth president doesn't just crave the approval of the electorate, as opposed to advancing policies he claimed were critical to the nation's welfare.

Read More:

- http://topics.nytimes.com/top/reference/timestopics/subjects/t/taxation/bush_tax_cuts/index.html
- http://www.taxpolicycenter.org/UploadedPDF/411749_updated_candidates.pdf
- http://www.politifact.com/truth-o-meter/promises/obameter/promise/38/repeal-the-bush-tax-cuts-for-higher-incomes/

REASON 45

MISERY LOVES COMPANY:
PLENTY OF BOTH

MAKING PRESIDENT CARTER LOOK
LIKE AN ECONOMIC GENIUS

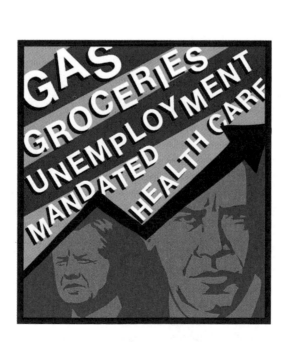

"Paychecks are flat and home values are falling. It's hard to pay for gas and groceries, and if you put it on a credit card, they've probably raised your rates. You're paying more than ever for health insurance that covers less and less. This isn't just a string of bad luck. The truth is that, while you've been living up to your responsibilities, Washington has not. That's why we need change. Real change."

—Candidate Barack Obama

Candidate Obama said he would solve the problems of flat paychecks, falling home values, and expensive gas and groceries while reducing the cost of our health insurance. President Obama's "solutions" brought us the highest unemployment rates in a generation, some of the highest mortgage defaults ever recorded, consistently declining home values, four-dollar-a-gallon gasoline, and food costs that are going up with no retreat in sight.

As for health care, Obama said, "You're paying more than ever for health insurance," so his solution was Obamacare: a mandated national health insurance program that forces you to buy into it or be fined.

What were Obama's words? "That's why we need change. Real change." We did get a change, but was it a change for the better?

The unemployment numbers are an example of an index, which is a measurement. There are other well-known indexes in addition to unemployment, such as housing starts and the misery index. The misery index is easy to calculate: the unemployment rate plus the inflation rate. Higher numbers mean stagflation, a combination of high joblessness and high prices.

The U.S. economy now has a misery index similar to that of the Carter administration. While the government statistics tell us unemployment is in the single digits and inflation is manageable, Americans know that nothing could be further from the truth on both counts. Americans are right.

Candidate Obama made promises to lower unemployment and gas prices, health care, and other basic costs. Unfortunately, his solutions brought us higher unemployment, more expensive gas, and mandated national health insurance.

After billions of dollars wasted on bailouts and stimulus plans and other measures, Americans may start to look back fondly on the Carter administration and remember those good old days.

An adage states "misery loves company." President Obama's interpretation may be "misery loves government," as he continues breaking promises to the American people.

Read More:

- *http://www.huffingtonpost.com/2008/09/17/obama-takes-on-economy-pa_n_127021.html*
- *http://www.miseryindex.us/customindexbymonth.asphttp://www.economicpolicyjournal.com/2011/05/shadow-stat-misery-index-highest-on.html*

SOMEBODY TELL
OPEC THE END IS NIGH

ENERGY POLICY GIVES OIL-PRODUCING
COUNTRIES A TRILLION DOLLARS A YEAR

OPEC
$1 TRILLION
IN EXPORT REVENUES

"It will be the policy of my administration to reverse our dependence on foreign oil while building a new energy economy that will create millions of jobs."

—President Barack Obama, six days after taking office

"We want to help you [Brazil] with the technology and support to develop these oil reserves safely, and when you're ready to start selling, we want to be one of your best customers."

—President Barack Obama, March 19, 2011

Apparently the best way to make money in the Obama economy is to have a river of oil beneath your feet. The *Financial Times* reported that business is booming for an organization that includes Iran, Libya, and Venezuela:

> The Organization of the Petroleum Exporting Countries (OPEC) is set to make a record-breaking $1 trillion in export revenues this year if crude oil prices remain above $100 a barrel, the International Energy Agency official told the *Financial Times*.

> "It would be the first time in the history of OPEC that oil revenues have reached a trillion dollars," Chief IEA Economist Fatih Birol told the *Financial Times*. "It's mainly because of higher prices and higher production."

For millions of Americans living from paycheck to paycheck, and for the millions more with no paycheck at all, this must be particularly cruel news—especially when much of OPEC's revenue increase can be attributed to the decline of the dollar and rising oil demand in emerging economies.

Countries lucky enough to have won the lottery in nature's dinosaur recycling program must look at the sun setting over the American Empire and wonder how our country could have fallen so far so fast.

President Obama blocks domestic oil production at every opportunity and aggressively fights incentives for petroleum exploration and production yet applauds the same exploration and production in foreign nations and commits to being one of their "best customers"—all while claiming to America that it's his policy to reverse our dependence on foreign oil.

Americans are left to wonder how a president with control of both houses of Congress failed to create a coherent energy policy that is more than hot air—particularly when he told voters he would.

Either the president is lying or his policy is a failure. Regardless, Americans are left with an empty tank as the cost of oil continues to soar and dollars are sent overseas to import the product.

Another promise to inspire hope and admiration; yet another promise broken.

Read More:

- *http://www.whitehouse.gov/blog_post/Fromperiltoprogress/*
- *http://www.bloomberg.com/news/2011-03-20/obama-tells-rousseff-he-wants-u-s-to-be-among-brazil-s-best-customers-.html*

WORDS DO MATTER, ESPECIALLY WHEN THEY'RE LIES!

ATTACKING HILLARY CLINTON ONLY TO PROVE HER RIGHT

"Don't tell me words don't matter!"

—Candidate Barack Obama
attacking Hillary Clinton, June 16, 2008

Both his admirers and foes admit that President Obama is an accomplished orator. With a rhythmic delivery, colorful prose, and an air of sincerity that soothes and persuades, he is ideally equipped to succeed in the political arena. Unfortunately, the polish of his words is not always matched by substance.

Hillary Clinton repeatedly attempted to undermine Obama's oratorical advantage when campaigning against him during the Democratic primary by pointing out that leadership requires solutions, not just speeches.

At one especially memorable point, Clinton suggested that the junior senator from Illinois needed a reality check because he was promising to solve so many of society's ills without actually offering any solutions.

Obama's response:

> Don't tell me words don't matter! "I have a dream," —just words? "We hold these truths to be self evident that all men are created equal," —just words ... just speeches?

Obama was correct; words do matter, when followed up by meaningful action.

As a candidate, Obama promised that

> • Obamacare "was not an individual mandate," but he lied. His signature legislation is a sweeping mandate requiring Americans to buy health insurance;

- he would end "warrantless wiretaps by the federal government," but he lied. Instead, he continued the Bush program, and then defended warrantless wiretapping in federal court in an effort to continue eavesdropping without oversight;

- he would "slash earmarks by more than half," but he lied. In reality, he allowed earmarks to increase, significantly;

- he would close the Guantánamo Bay detention facility, but he lied. Not only did he keep Guantánamo open, but he also began military tribunals there;

- he would increase the minimum wage to $9.50 by 2011, but he lied. At last check, it's still $7.25.

Those five items are just a few examples of his runaway hypocrisy and willingness to say anything, to any audience, to get a reaction and win support.

Obama's words do matter, and his deeds matter even more. Sadly, his words too often ring hollow, and his deeds run directly counter to his promises. If only the American people had been wise enough to heed Hillary Clinton's warning.

Four years after our voting mistake, here's hoping the American people vote for action and not just empty words, this time around.

Read More:

- http://www.nytimes.com/2008/02/18/us/politics/18video.html
- http://abcnews.go.com/blogs/politics/2008/02/obama-rebuts-cl/
- http://www.youtube.com/watch?v=t6NS9unm-OQ

FINALLY HAVE A JOB INTERVIEW? PRETEND IT'S TAKE-YOUR-KID-TO-WORK DAY

AFTER PROMISES OF AID FOR JOB SEEKERS NEEDING CHILD CARE, OBAMA IGNORES THE UNEMPLOYED

Benefits Promised

*Refundable credit

Non-Refundable Credit

50%

Harsh Reality

*Current Refundable Credit

Current Non-Refundable Credit

65%

35%

"[Senator Obama promised to make the child and dependent care tax credit available to] individuals paying for child care needed so they can either work or look for work. Senator Obama's tax plan would make the credit refundable and increase the maximum rate from 35 to 50 percent."

— analysis of Candidate Obama's tax plan

Before the 2008 election, Candidate Obama accused Senator McCain of abandoning unemployed workers and single-parent households by not proposing to expand child care tax credits for those struggling financially.

He also proposed his own solution: to expand financial aid for those paying for child or dependent care, allowing people to work or look for work.

According to the Brookings Institution, perhaps the most recognized liberal think tank, Candidate Obama promised to make the child and dependent care tax credit available to

> individuals paying for child care needed so they can either work or look for work. Senator Obama's tax plan would make the credit refundable and increase the maximum rate from 35 to 50 percent. It would also increase from $15,000 to $30,000 the threshold at which the credit rate begins to phase down and reduce the rate by 2 percentage points (rather than the current 1) for each $2,000 or fraction thereof above that level.

Obama's manipulation of political issues was masterful during the election. His strategy depended largely on successfully wooing suburban women who tend to support Republicans.

To win these voters, Obama attacked McCain on emotional issues that resonate with suburban women. In particular, he attacked

McCain over his failure to propose help for those paying for child care or dependent care (usually women) to whom Obama's target voters could relate.

Obama ingratiated himself with this critical bloc of voters by assuring them he would increase the tax credit to 50 percent and make it refundable. Those who pay for child or dependent care would thus get a substantial return from the government.

Unfortunately for the Brookings Institution, the legions of suburban women Obama targeted for votes, and the low-income and unemployed parents of dependent children, President Obama has not kept the promise he made as Candidate Obama.

With disturbingly high unemployment during the president's first three years in office, many single parents who fit the looking-for-work description have been left out in the cold by yet another broken promise from Candidate Obama.

Read More:

- *http://www.taxpolicycenter.org/UploadedPDF/411749_updated_candidates.pdf*
- *http://www.politifact.com/truth-o-meter/promises/obameter/promise/10/expand-the-child-and-dependent-care-credit/*

TWO FACES:
ONE AS CANDIDATE,
ANOTHER AS PRESIDENT

IGNORING HIS OWN HYPOCRISY
WITH LATINO VOTERS

Pants-on-Fire rating for Candidate Obama's campaign commercial, targeting Latino votes for his benefit.

—PolitiFact.com, a group that conducts nonpartisan political analysis

"It is a cynical ploy to try to drive Latino votes to benefit a Republican candidate."

—President Barack Obama

In the days leading up to the 2008 presidential election, Candidate Obama ran a Spanish-language commercial titled *Two Faces*. Obama's claims about Senator McCain's immigration stance were so deceitful that a Pulitzer Prize-winning, nonpartisan, fact-checking group gave it what it calls a Pants-on-Fire label. This commercial was a clear example of a politician attempting to divide voters and polarize opinion by advancing a falsehood about his opponent.

Now fast-forward two years into President Obama's term, when a controversial Spanish-language commercial was run against Democrat Harry Reid in Nevada urging Latinos not to vote at all since Senate Majority Leader Reid had not advanced immigration reform.

It was almost comical to hear President Obama's harsh take on the newer commercial, given his willingness as a candidate to deceive and divide in pursuit of votes: "It is a cynical political ploy to try to drive Latino votes to benefit a Republican candidate."

The president correctly identified the ad's cynicism but failed to admit his own hypocrisy in attacking Republicans for doing a strikingly similar thing he did just two years earlier.

Candidate Obama's commercial titled *Two Faces* was in reference to John McCain, his Republican opponent. But his about-face as president concerning a very similar commercial run against a Democrat makes it clear that President Obama also deserves the moniker Two-Faced.

It may be difficult even for Obama to top this hypocrisy, but with the 2012 campaign underway, he may do just that.

Read More:

- *http://www.politifact.com/truth-o-meter/statements/2008/sep/19/barack-obama/limbaughs-not-a-mccain-spokesman/*
- *http://blogs.abcnews.com/politicalpunch/2008/09/from-the-fact-1.html*
- *http://blogs.wsj.com/washwire/2010/10/19/dont-vote-ads-aimed-at-latinos-are-pulled-in-nevada/*
- *http://www.cbsnews.com/8301-503544_162-5097178-503544.html*

PROMISED AID TO AMERICANS WITH DISABILITIES—MAYBE NEXT ELECTION

PLAYING BOTH SIDES, ONLY TO FAIL THEM BOTH

EQUAL
OPPORTUNITY?

AMERICAN DREAM

"As president, Barack Obama will announce the creation of a National Commission on People with Disabilities ... examining and proposing solutions to work disincentives in the SSDI, SSI, Medicare, and Medicaid programs."

"[I promise to] provide preferences in federal contracting to small businesses owned by members of socially and economically disadvantaged groups to include individuals with disabilities."

—Candidate Barack Obama

In a brilliant political maneuver, Candidate Obama promised to create a national commission to examine whether government grant programs like Medicaid, Medicare, Social Security Disability Insurance and others provided to disabled citizens are so generous that they discourage them from working.

This one promise appealed to two critical voter groups: one swayed by a heart-stirring commitment to defend the disabled and the other consisting of fiscal conservatives concerned that federal benefits might be a disincentive for Americans with disabilities to work.

All Obama had to do was announce the creation of a national commission to keep his promise. But either that announcement was too great to keep or the promise too insincere.

"Fifty-four million Americans—roughly one in six—personally experience some form of disability…Yet seventeen years after Congress enacted the Americans with Disabilities Act (ADA), Americans with disabilities still do not have an equal opportunity to fulfill the American Dream," said Candidate Obama.

With the stroke of a pen he could have created a national commission to examine the possibility that government grants have provided a disincentive to work.

Tackling obstacles to the American Dream are proven campaign fodder, but this particular promise carried the heft of common sense within an ongoing social and political debate.

Even the nonpartisan PolitiFact group registered its disappointment:

> After electronic searches through Whitehouse.gov, Google, and Nexis, we haven't found any tangible activity on this promise during the past year. The White House was unable to provide any evidence that progress on this promise is being made.

Having used the disabled in America to successfully appeal to two sides of an ideological divide, President Obama not only disappointed them both, but also failed the fifty-four million disabled who stood to benefit.

His other promise—to aid those with disabilities by directing his agency to provide "preferences in federal contracting" to them— is yet another example of Obama promising something to get our vote, then failing to keep his promise once elected.

This promise was shockingly simple to keep. The Small Business Administration (SBA) is within the executive branch.

As president he is the leader of the executive branch. President Obama appointed the head of the SBA. He could have easily directed the SBA to help those with disabilities, as he promised.

But he didn't.

When Obama was seeking our votes he was direct, passionate, and fervent in his commitment to help Americans with disabilities. So much so that even after choosing Joe Biden as his running mate, he printed campaign material highlighting their promise.

Barack Obama and Joe Biden would direct the Small Business Administration to amend regulations under the Small Business Act that provide preferences in federal contracting to small businesses owned by members of socially and economically disadvantaged groups to include individuals with disabilities.

Unfortunately, Candidate Obama's words are only that: words. As president, Obama failed to act on either of his promises to help Americans with disabilities.

The litany of broken promises continues. Growing legions of Americans gullibly traded Obama's words for votes, but no one was more harmed by Obama's failure to act on these matters than the fifty-four million disabled Americans to whom he promised so much but delivered so little.

Read More:

- http://www.barackobama.com/pdf/DisabilityPlanFactSheet.pdf
- http://www.sba.gov/category/advocacy-navigation-structure/about-us
- http://www.thearc.org/document.doc?id=3073
- http://www.politifact.com/truth-o-meter/promises/obameter/ promise/98/change-federal-rules-so-small-businesses-owned-by-/
- http://www.politifact.com/truth-o-meter/promises/obameter/ promise/97/create-a-national-commission-on-people-with-disabi/

THERE'S TOO MUCH MONEY IN POLITICS, UNLESS IT'S CONTRIBUTED TO ME!

OBAMA FLIP-FLOPS ON SUPER-PACS AND BREAKS PLEDGE TO HONOR PUBLIC FUNDING OF PRESIDENTIAL CAMPAIGN

"Super-PACs are 'a threat to democracy.' [Super-PACs have a] corrosive influence of money in politics."

—President Barack Obama

In the television age political campaigns rise and fall on advertising dollars, mostly bestowed upon candidates by their supporters. These dollars not only affect the outcome of elections but also make critics wonder what influence they've purchased in the process. That is why the federal government imposes contribution limits, and even spending caps, in the case of its matching funds.

In 2008 President Obama pronounced his intention to accept matching funds and their accompanying limits. However, when his contribution totals began to rise, he jettisoned his pledge and went on a fundraising and spending spree.

In an article about Obama's about-face, *The New York Times* wrote:

> In making its decision to bypass public financing, the campaign declined an infusion of $84.1 million in money from federal taxpayers...

> To make the exchange worthwhile, aides said, Mr. Obama would need to raise at least twice as much money than he would have received under public financing, with a goal of raising three times as much.

After riding a tidal wave of campaign cash into office, President Obama had the audacity to chastise the U.S. Supreme Court during his 2011 State of the Union speech after the court held that unlimited corporate contributions equal free speech.

This unprecedented attack during a State of the Union address led one justice to shake his head, signifying no, while mouthing the words, "that's not true." A senator from Obama's own party said, "Maybe those weren't appropriate" in reference to the president's comments.

Surprisingly (or, in keeping with his usual approach if you've been paying attention), President Obama recently responded to low polling numbers and slower political contributions by reversing field and welcoming the resources of a super-PAC formed to support his campaign.

If this reads like the definition of hypocrisy and audacity, well, it is. Even the *Washington Post* had this to say on the flip-flop:

> The principled position he took on super-PACs was one of the strongest he's taken on any issue to date—"threat to democracy" is pretty strong language—and his new position is set to push the bounds of what's a permissible relationship between a super-PAC and a campaign.
>
> His campaign announced Monday that not only is it okay with what Priorities USA is doing, but that it will dispatch campaign officials, White House staff, and even cabinet officials to Priorities USA events—though it should be noted that they will not actively ask for donations to the super-PAC, which would be illegal.
>
> Obama, in effect, is signaling that he is not just ready to play the game but that he is ready to game the system as well.

The 180-degree flip-flops of Obama's beliefs on campaign financing make suspect his repeated criticisms that so much money in the political system is "corrosive" or that super-PACs are "a threat to democracy."

Both may be true, but equally true is that such flagrant hypocrisy and gross rejection of stated beliefs is corrosive of America's faith in our elected officials.

Whether he raises $1 billion or not, Obama's repeatedly broken promises to voters may be a much greater threat to democracy.

Read More:

- *http://www.washingtonpost.com/politics/obama-in-a-switch-endorses-pro-democratic-super-pac/2012/02/06/glQAVqnWvQ_story.html*
- *http://www.nytimes.com/2008/06/20/us/politics/20obama.html?pagewanted=all*
- *http://cnsnews.com/news/article/dem-senator-obama-s-attack-supreme-court-last-year-s-sotu-may-not-have-been-appropriate*

REASON 52

HE PROMISED HOPE AND LEADERSHIP BUT DELIVERED HOPELESSNESS AND FAILURE

OBAMA PROMISED TO LEAD ON DEBT, THE DISABLED, GENOCIDE, AND MANY OTHER POLICIES... BUT FAILED

LEADERSHIP FAILURE

"[R]aising the debt limit is a sign of leadership failure."

—U.S. Senator Barack Obama

As a senator and candidate for president, Obama viciously attacked his opponents and the establishment for their failures to lead. Perhaps this is no more evident than in the case of the national debt.

With a smile and a sharp tongue Senator Obama criticized many over a host of politically volatile issues, from congressional earmarks to immigration reform and voting to raise the debt ceiling. Yet once elected president, Obama staked out some of the same positions without hesitation or any sense of hypocrisy.

This may be one of history's greatest examples of failure in leadership.

Candidate Obama was quick to attack his opponents and the status quo over failures on congressional earmarks, the Armenian genocide, the disabled, the national debt, the debt ceiling, immigration reform, and many of his opponent's other leadership failures.

Remember Obama's partisan attack, and his promise to slash congressional earmarks "to less than $7.8 billion a year, the level they were at before 1994, when the Republicans took control of Congress?"

And we can't forget Obama's poignant partisanship on the debt-ceiling vote:

The fact that we are here today to debate raising America's debt limit is a sign of leadership failure … Leadership means that "the buck stops here." Instead, Washington is shifting the burden of bad choices today onto the backs of our children and grandchildren. America has a debt problem and a failure of leadership. Americans deserve better. I therefore intend to oppose the effort to increase America's debt limit (March 16, 2006).

President Obama continued attacking politicians once elected, only this time he attacked them for holding the same positions he had before he became president.

As a senator, Obama said, "I always believe that ultimately, if people are paying attention, then we get good government and good leadership. And when we get lazy as a democracy, and civically start taking shortcuts, then it results in bad government and politics."

It's time for the voters to pay attention to President Obama's leadership failure. The difficulties we face as a nation are too great to tolerate four more years of lies and hypocrisy.

Read More:

- *http://www.cbsnews.com/8301-503544_162-20027412-503544.html*
- *http://www.nationalreview.com/corner/256199/obama-not-always-fan-upping-debt-ceiling-katrina-trinko*
- *http://www.barackobama.com/pdf/issues/fiscal/ObamaPolicy_Fiscal.pdf*